2016-17 BIG BASH BOOK

KFC BBL

rebel WBBL

2016–17 BIG BASH BOOK

Go behind the scenes, meet the teams for the upcoming season, and relive the best moments of BBL|05 and WBBL|01

Daniel Lane

ALLEN & UNWIN
SYDNEY • MELBOURNE • AUCKLAND • LONDON

CONTENTS

WELCOME TO THE KFC BIG BASH LEAGUE

One of the greatest signs of the impact the KFC Big Bash League's fifth instalment had on cricket was former national captain Steve Waugh teaching young players at one of his coaching clinics the nuances of the reverse sweep—a shot he'd learnt from watching the likes of the Sydney Sixers' Nic Maddinson. Regarded as a custodian of the sport's noble traditions—Waugh is acknowledged as the Test skipper who brought a new-found respect to Australia's baggy green cap—the then 50-year-old was comfortable teaching the group how to play a shot that, along with the ramp, has added to the zing 'n' bling of a typical night at the BBL.

'I would've loved to have played T20,' said Waugh. 'It's exciting watching [the BBL] develop, and it seems there's a new shot being played in every game. I think it's a format that really tests a batsman out, but if you're good enough you can play all the shots. I think if you practise it, a reverse sweep is no more dangerous than a cut shot.'

With kids around the nation wearing Perth Scorchers shirts, waving Adelaide Strikers flags, banging together Sydney Sixers thundersticks, lining up for selfies with Hobart's mascot Captain Hurricane, adopting players such as the Brisbane Heat's big hitter Chris Lynn or Sydney Thunder's Clint McKay as their favourite cricketer or following the Melbourne Renegades or Stars with a passion traditionally reserved for AFL teams, Waugh acknowledged the grip the BBL has on

generation-next by formulating T20-specific clinics.

'You need to teach kids how to play the shots they're seeing and also to do things like bowl slower-ball bumpers and how to think differently at the end of a game during the death overs,' he said of life as a BBL-era cricket clinic coordinator.

BBL|05 built on the outrageous success of the previous summer with record television ratings, record club membership numbers and jaw-dropping crowd figures, including the 80,883 who watched the Stars–Renegades derby at the MCG. 'To have [a crowd that size] will send shock waves around the cricketing world as to just where T20 sits,' observed Stars coach and former New Zealand international Stephen Fleming.

Indeed, the demand for the fast and furious form of cricket has led to suggestions that in future a BBL game could be staged on Christmas Day. It's a far cry from the alarm that led to the creation of the league when a Cricket Australia survey had boys aged under 15 ranking cricket their seventh favourite sport, while girls the same age placed it 14th.

The league, and the formation of the highly successful Rebel Women's Big Bash League in 2015–16, led to what the BBL's chief executive Mike McKenna described as an 'explosion' of kids playing the game and, just as importantly, it's providing an audience whose passion for cricket ought to grow over the years. 'They're going to help underwrite the future of the game,' said McKenna during a summer when BBL matches regularly attracted more than a million television viewers to make it the highest rating league on Australian television.

Sydney Sixers fast bowler Doug Bollinger said one of the joys of playing in the BBL was seeing the nature of the crowds flocking to stadiums for their fix of high-octane, adrenaline-charged cricket. 'The BBL is bringing families together,' he said. 'They're feeling the atmosphere, seeing the fireworks, the fours, the sixes, wickets, and it's a shared experience and that becomes a shared interest.'

And they had plenty to cheer, courtesy of the 131 players who competed in the crash 'n' bash of the BBL. The numbers tell the tale of a summer no one wanted to end:

- 1,030,494 people turned out to the 35 matches, an increase of 206,665 on BBL|04.
- 29,442 was the average BBL attendance, an increase of 6000 on the previous season.
- 11,013 total runs were scored, 875 more than in BBL|04.
- 412 wickets were taken—down 12 on the previous summer.
- 117 metres was the distance the Hurricanes' Daniel Christian's six travelled from his bat to the roof at the Gabba.
- 376 sixes were hit.
- 27 sixes were smashed by the Brisbane Heat's Chris Lynn.
- 18 wickets were taken by the Thunder's Clint McKay, the most of the competition.
- Five centuries were hit in the tournament, two of them were struck by Usman Khawaja.
- 8.19 runs per over were scored throughout the tournament, up from 7.82 in BBL|04.
- 56 runs were scored by Travis Head off the last 15 balls of the innings when Adelaide beat the Sixers on New Year's Eve.
- 11 runs—the least amount scored off a bowler's four overs—were conceded by Chris Tremain of the Renegades and Daniel Worrell of the Stars.

Daniel Lane

ADAM GILCHRIST ON BBL|05

THE MAGICAL NIGHT THE BBL BECAME BIG!

I think those of us who believe in the KFC Big Bash League had our 'Kerry Packer/World Series Cricket' moment on 2 January 2016—the evening when 80,883 spectators attended the MCG to watch the Melbourne derby.

After the public failed to support World Series Cricket in its inaugural year, Kerry Packer realised in November 1978 when the SCG staged its first day–night game that his vision had a future. So many people had queued along Driver Avenue to watch cricket under lights the media giant ordered for the gates to be swung open to let them all in.

The rise and rise of the BBL hasn't been quite as dramatic because, unlike World Series Cricket, it is controlled by the sport's governing body. However, since its inception there have been some critics who have derided it as 'not cricket', 'crash 'n' bash' and 'hit 'n' giggle'—the same accusations that were launched at Packer's so-called 'circus' all those years ago.

I was in Perth preparing to commentate on the Scorchers–Sixers match as part of Network Ten's double-header Saturday night over the New Year's weekend, and there was a special buzz among the team to know we were beaming around the world fantastic vision of the MCG packed with mums, dads and kids for a domestic T20 game.

In my opinion 2 January 2016 is cemented as a BBL 'icon day' because while the nightly television ratings throughout the season of one million-plus viewers has stunned television executives, the presence of 80,883 fans at the game confirmed the belief a few of us share that the Big Bash is now an essential thread in the fabric of an Australian summer.

Some people thought the league may have peaked in BBL|04 with the record crowds, bumper television ratings and a brand of cricket that needed to be seen to be believed; however, the events of BBL|05 suggest the League will only get bigger, bolder and brasher in the years to come.

The key to the success is the players, and when I reflect upon the summer of 2015–16, I recall the excitement I felt on New Year's Eve when Travis Head of the Strikers sent almost 50,000 people at Adelaide Oval into raptures by blasting 56 runs off the last 15 balls he faced to reach a century and guide his team to an unlikely win. It was epic, and when I recall that night I remember how special it was to see a massive crowd erupt and celebrate the sheer joy and sense of fun cricket provides.

There are many other moments from BBL|05 that are embedded in the memory bank: young Jake Lehmann hitting the first ball he faced as a BBL player—the last delivery of the game—for six to win the match; Jacques Kallis bowling an incredible final over to secure a one-run win for the Thunder over the Stars; Usman Khawaja's breathtaking summer of runs; Brisbane's Chris Lynn smashing five consecutive sixes; Chris Gayle's 12-ball half century for the Renegades; the young fellow in the crowd who ate his way through a watermelon—rind and all—and, of course, a showreel's worth of classic catches.

And I'm lucky enough to be in the commentary box for Network Ten calling the action! When people ask me what that's like, I answer it's exciting, it's hectic but, most of all, it's a great deal of fun—and I love it.

The BBL produces a brand of cricket that lends itself to animated support and good old-fashioned barracking. My fellow commentators Ricky Ponting, Damien Fleming, Mark Waugh and Mark Howard are mindful of not screaming over the top and making noise for noise's sake—but sometimes it is hard to contain the raw roar of approval for something spectacular . . . like Travis Head's incredible knock.

Just like the viewer at home we also ride the rollercoaster of emotion but something Punter, Flemo, Junior, Howie and I appreciate is we can't try to control the show, the cricket controls the show and as commentators we have to simply go with it. The quality of the cricket is what sells the Big Bash to the public and our aim is simply to add some interesting points and enhance the viewers' experience.

We've dug deep to add more expert opinion to BBL|06 with Australian coach Darren Lehmann joining Andrew Symonds, Brendon McCullum and Mel Jones in the commentary box, while the respected journalist Roz Kelly will come on board as co-host.

BBL|05 was another watershed moment in the rise and rise of the T20 game but I firmly believe the best is still to come. And based on what we've already seen . . . and marvelled at . . . that's an exciting thought.

Adam Gilchrist

PRAISE NOT PUNCHES . . .

SAYING GOODBYE TO MIKE HUSSEY

When Melbourne Stars captain David Hussey bowled to his older brother, the Sydney Thunder's skipper Mike Hussey, during the BBL|05 Big Final, one thing he knew wouldn't happen at the MCG was their mother needing to break up yet another fight.

The brothers played their childhood backyard cricket matches in Perth with such a ferocity it didn't take much more than a bouncer hitting its mark or a refusal to abide by the automatic 'wickie' rule for a game to erupt into a fight.

'Mike would chase me and it would end up in fisticuffs,' recalled David, two years Mike's junior, of their wars. 'They really were heated affairs because he wanted to get me out and I wanted to get him out and as we grew older the competition levels only increased.'

That competitiveness was definitely still there when Mike, playing in his final game of an outstanding career, walked out to bat at the MCG with the Thunder on course to win the crown—and to complete a cricket fairytale of transforming from the league's easybeats into world-beaters.

Despite the high stakes, David proved there was room for brotherly love—and respect—for a valiant foe when he directed the Stars to acknowledge the 40-year-old's status in the game by forming a guard of honour. Their mother, who was celebrating her birthday that night, would have smiled when she saw the pair shake hands—rather than raise their fists—seconds before Mike took strike. 'It was nice. It wasn't something I was expecting—a guard of honour,' Mike Hussey said of the heart-warming gesture. 'It was a nice touch.'

He wasn't surprised, though, to see his younger brother, a seasoned Australian one-day international player, warming up to bowl for the first time in two years. '[It was] a smart tactic really, as you don't want to get out to your brother, particularly in your last game,' said Mike. 'I had a feeling that he might do it.'

Hussey, one of Australian cricket's best loved players, scored 18 before Adam Zampa bowled him with 39 runs needed for victory. His first reaction was disappointment, but as he walked off the ground he took the time to absorb the sight of the crowd affording him a standing ovation. 'As I was coming off I was annoyed with myself for playing such a silly shot at that stage of the game,' he said, 'but I did think to myself, "I've just got to take a few moments to soak this in." '

Ben Rohrer sealed the victory—and the trophy—by hitting a six down the ground. As he ran to celebrate with his teammates, Rohrer felt pleased to see his captain's face. 'Hitting the winning runs was a magic moment, but seeing the joy of Huss's face to be going out a winner was special,' he said. 'I could see what it meant to him.'

The victory justified Hussey's decision to leave the ultra-successful Perth Scorchers for a franchise dismissed as a 'basket case' after finishing the first three BBL tournaments in last place. Hussey joined forces with chief

Getty Images

executive Nick Cummins and coach Paddy Upton to develop a blueprint to ensure the Thunder resonated, but as fireworks exploded above the MCG to celebrate his team's triumph, Hussey seemed surprised that success had come so soon. 'This is what you plan for,' he said. 'This is what you hope to achieve, but when you actually do it . . . it takes a bit of time to sink in. It's been a long journey. It's taken a long time and there have been a few heartaches along the way. But to actually reach the summit with the group of guys has been a reward for a lot of hard work.'

When asked what he hoped his legacy would be at the Thunder, Hussey spoke from the heart. 'I think a good work ethic, to be able to stay calm under pressure, and it's important to have good players, but it's equally as important to have good characters in a successful team,' he said. 'That's certainly what we've tried to bestow on our players—to win humbly, be modest, be respectful of the game and be respectful of each other.'

And there was no greater example of that respectfulness than when the Hussey boys set their rivalry aside for a few seconds to acknowledge that their bond as brothers counted for something special amid the drama of a final.

'FOR MIKE, MY BROTHER. YOU WON TONIGHT. YOU GOT THE CHOCOLATES. YOU'VE BEEN FANTASTIC YOUR WHOLE CRICKETING CAREER. YOU'RE AN ICON OF THE GAME AND A TRUE REFLECTION OF HOW PEOPLE SHOULD BE PLAYING THE GAME . . .'

—Melbourne Stars captain David Hussey's tribute to his brother Mike after the BBL|05 Big Final

SECRETS OF THE X-FACTOR

A GIFT FROM SANTA

TIM LUDEMAN

ADELAIDE STRIKERS
Opening batsman/wicketkeeper

Describe your role at the Adelaide Strikers.

I'm an aggressive top-order batsman and wicketkeeper. When you bat in the powerplay you have to make as many runs as possible to provide a decent platform for the next guys coming in, like Travis Head and Brad Hodge. It's a fun role to have.

How do you cope with the pressure of playing in a BBL match?

I suppose when you get into the zone you don't really feel it. You focus so hard on the ball nothing else matters, but in between deliveries, when you get a little bit of downtime, you soak it all in because the Adelaide crowd is mad about T20 cricket and the Strikers. It's brilliant to be a part of it.

What's your approach to training?

I think most players would train in similar ways, but I think what can differ is the way you go about it, the intensity and the way we challenge [ourselves] to be better players.

Who's been a good mentor for you?

I've had a few over the years. When I was quite young, Ian 'Lefty' Wright from Warrnambool was someone I learnt from. His approach was to give 100 percent to whatever he was doing, and Stephen Field also helped me out a lot back then. My family were obviously very supportive, while [former Strikers coach] Darren Berry was tremendous, especially with the wicketkeeping side of the game. They were all very honest. A lot of people will tell you what you want to hear, but a good mentor has heart-to-heart conversations and they ensure your head is clear so you can perform at your best.

What is the best present you ever received?

When I was nine or 10 years old, Santa Claus left a pair of wicketkeeping gloves and pads for me under the Christmas tree, and that was the greatest present ever. It changed my life.

What's your motto?

It's just to have fun. I know that's simple, but fun is why you play sport, and if you lose sight of that you're probably in it for the wrong reasons.

TAKE IT AS IT COMES

CHRIS LYNN

BRISBANE HEAT
Batsman

Describe your role at the Brisbane Heat.

To hit the ball into the crowd and score as many runs as possible. I took on a new role during BBL|05; I was a first-time captain, so my job was to lead the boys around the park. I didn't see 'leading' as talking in the change room; I thought it was important to lead by my actions.

Do you specifically practise your big hits at training?

I believe in training as you'll play, and my mindset going into a net session is very similar to how I'll go into a game. I like to get in some range-hitting out in the middle of the Gabba. As cricketers, we're very grateful to be able to [train] on the middle of the wicket and 'bomb' the ball as far as we can, to figure out the distances to different boundaries. I think in any situation you want to take the positive route—no matter what it is.

At what age did you realise you could hit the ball further than other kids?

Trying to whack the ball is what lured me into cricket. It was the reason why I wanted to bat from a young age. I realised the more runs you scored, the more opportunities you had to whack the ball out of the park. To me, that's the fun you have in cricket. As a young cricketer I wasn't one to be patient at the crease or to hang around. I wanted fun, and for me that was fours and sixes.

Who was your inspiration?

You can pick any of the Australian players from back in the day. I loved watching Ricky Ponting and Adam Gilchrist, but it was also exciting to see guys like Brett Lee bat. While he was a fast bowler, whenever Brett had the opportunity to bat he just crunched the ball. Watching A.B. de Villiers, Chris Gayle and Dave Warner is special. They're so far ahead of the game in the modern era; it's them, daylight and then the rest of the field.

What's your personal motto?

Whatever will be will be. I've found that whenever I put pressure on myself I tend to fail, so I say, 'Whatever will be will be,' to get through the game and to enjoy it for what it is.

THE REALITY OF RUNS

BEN DUNK

HOBART HURRICANES

Batsman

Getty Images

Describe your role with the Hobart Hurricanes.

I'm an opening batsman and last season I was the team's vice-captain. That means one part of my role is to go out and get the team off to as quick a start as possible during the power-play. As the vice-captain I was there to help our skipper Tim Paine because he had a big job wicketkeeping, opening the batting and captaining the team.

There must be a lot of stress knowing you have to score those quick runs in the powerplay.

There's pressure and the expectation is you'll score above 50 in those six overs. Sometimes if the wicket is a little bit sticky or is playing well for the 'quicks' it can be difficult. However, the reality is that regardless of the wicket you're expected to get the team off to as good a start as possible.

There are big names at the Hurricanes—how's it feel kitting up alongside Kumar Sangakkara, Shaun Tait, George Bailey and Tim Paine?

Amazing! I reckon it would've been every boy's dream to play alongside Sangakkara because he's one of the game's genuine greats. It's surreal but when you're opening the batting and know one of the world's best [batters] is coming in after you, it gives some licence to play shots because you want him to come out and face as many balls as he possibly can.

What did you learn from Sangakkara and how has it helped you?

I learnt he goes through the same struggles as everybody else; for instance, a lack of confidence when he's down on runs. He has the same battles as every cricketer and that was an eye-opener because you put someone with Kumar's record on a pedestal. It was refreshing for a battler like myself to see even the best in the world struggle sometimes.

Is there a particular story you gain inspiration from?

Growing up in Far North Queensland during an era when Queensland was a dominant force in the Sheffield Shield, I looked at Jimmy Maher as a trailblazer. He came from my hometown of Innisfail and, by representing Australia, Jimmy proved to all the young players in the region that it could be done.

Do you have a personal motto?

Not really. I'm fully aware I am very lucky to do what I do for a living because not many people get the opportunity.

PUSH BEYOND YOUR COMFORT ZONE

Getty Images

NICK WINTER

MELBOURNE RENEGADES

Bowler

Describe your role in the team.

Despite being one of the younger members of the Renegades, I feel my role is to be aggressive with the new ball and try to maximise wicket-taking opportunities for the team. If we're able to dictate from the start, we go a long way to winning the game. In saying that, at a young age I still enjoy sitting back and observing how the more experienced players like James Pattinson and Peter Siddle go about their work.

What's the most nerve-racking aspect of the BBL and how do you cope with it?

T20 carries significant pressure for all involved, as its fast-paced nature means the course of a game can change off one ball. Especially with the Melbourne derbies attracting combined crowds of 120,000 last season, players need to be ready to cope with being put in the spotlight. For me, it's a case of trying to relax at the top of my mark and blocking out the surrounding environment, because that's irrelevant in the contest between bat and ball.

Describe your approach to training.

I'm lucky that the Renegades have several high-quality coaches and assistants across all aspects, so training for me is all about quality and trying to improve. It's key to make sure that I'm confident in my skills heading into game day, and from a bowling perspective I've executed the deliveries that I'll use in a match. Despite being a short game, fitness is also crucial in T20, with intense running with each ball—so I stay on top of my conditioning.

How important is to have a plan B in T20?

The nature of T20 cricket and the growing ability of batsmen to hit to any part of the ground means we bowlers must be able to adapt immediately to a situation on the field. One of the Renegades' priorities is that each bowler is capable of several bowling deliveries and tactics that we can rely on in high pressure situations.

Is there a story that inspires you?

There's no particular story that motivates me as such, it's more the thought that I have an opportunity not many have, so that continues to drive me towards being the best I can be.

What's your personal motto?

Life begins at the end of your comfort zone.

TAKE THE GAME ON

MEG LANNING

MELBOURNE STARS

Batter

Describe your role at the Melbourne Stars.

It was a great honour to captain the Stars in the first WBBL. It was an exciting time for women's cricket, and to be my team's skipper was very special.

How do you cope with the pressure of a WBBL game?

It's obviously very important as the team's leader to play well and to get the team off to a good start, so I go into every game expecting to perform and make runs. It's important you treat each game differently and try to 'spark' every time. Sometimes it works, sometimes it doesn't, but that's just the way cricket goes.

What's your approach to training?

I think it's important to train how you're going to play, get into really good habits by practising how you want to perform out in the middle. The idea is to put yourself in possible match situations [at training] because it means you should be prepared to deal with those scenarios when they occur in a game—and hopefully the outcome will be good.

How do you think your approach to cricket differs from other players?

I try to take the game on as much as I can. I try to take it to the bowlers, and I've found if you can get on top of the battle early—hit a few boundaries—it really puts the pressure back on them. I think the key is to put your opponent under pressure so you can play your natural game.

What, or who, inspired you to get involved in sport?

My parents played a lot of sport, and they were responsible for getting me involved in sport and cricket. Dad played a lot of cricket when he was younger, and when he'd watch the game on television I would sit next to him. That was where I gained my inspiration to play.

Do you have a personal motto?

I know it will sound clichéd but it's just to go out and have fun. I started playing cricket because I enjoyed the game, it was a lot of fun, and it's still very much the same today. I believe the more you embrace that idea of playing for fun and enjoyment, the better you'll be.

Getty Images

STAY TRUE BLUE

JASON BEHRENDORFF

PERTH SCORCHERS
Fast bowler

Describe your role at the Perth Scorchers.

I open the bowling, and something we talk about at the WACA [aka #TheFurnace] is swinging the ball. That's an important part of our game plan, and I try to take early wickets because they help get us on the front foot.

Sum up your approach to training.

I train with a purpose because there's no point in just getting through a session. In terms of the Big Bash, we bowl four overs and every ball is crucial—there's no time to warm into it. You have to hit the ground running, and I train with the intensity needed for that.

Whose approach to cricket has made a positive impression on you?

Alfonso Thomas [from South Africa] was one of the Scorchers' overseas imports [in BBL|02], and his philosophy was you practised at training so when you're out in the middle you have the confidence needed to do things like bowl a wide yorker.

You played with a stress fracture in your back last summer. How tough was that?

It's hard, and I needed to learn to do it. I'm the first to admit I was a bowler who'd tell everyone I was sore. You learn the difference between 'good soreness' and 'bad soreness' and most of the time you have to play through the good soreness. Last year I played in the BBL with a stress fracture—that's what we call bad soreness. It took a lot of mental energy to get myself up for each game, because I knew every time I bowled I'd be sore. However, I had the hunger and passion to bowl and I wanted to be an asset to the team. When you break through a barrier [like that] it gives you a belief you can push through things. It makes you a stronger person and a stronger cricketer.

What is your personal motto?

There's an old adage I like—Work hard and gain respect—but I also focus on continued improvement and staying true to myself. Staying true to yourself is something you develop over a period of time, but it's something that is a part of my Christian faith. A good way to describe it is that it's your value system—sticking to your values and not being pressured to do something that isn't aligned to the way you go about life.

DON'T PLAY SCARED

BRAD HADDIN

SYDNEY SIXERS
Wicketkeeper/batsman

Getty Images

Describe your role in the Sixers.

My role is to be the best player possible. I don't have any extra roles at the Sixers now, but when the team started I was lucky enough to be captain. I was the first player signed to the Sixers and I spent a lot of time with Stuart Clark, who was our general manager, and coach Trevor Bayliss creating a list that would sustain us over a long period of time. That's something I'm very proud of.

How do you cope with the pressure of BBL?

I enjoy it! I think the [KFC] Big Bash League has been a great innovation by Cricket Australia and the people responsible should be proud of what they've established. It has allowed younger players the opportunity to play under pressure in front of big crowds, and that holds them in good stead leading into their international career.

What is your approach to training?

You can't go into a T20 tournament underdone. You need to make sure your fitness and power are spot on because if you just rolled in [to the BBL] you risk injuries because it's such a high-paced brand of cricket. The fitter you are the better decisions you make under pressure, and in T20 the whole game is played under pressure.

Is there a story that motivates you?

I look at what my daughter Mia went through [a one in 100,000 battle with a rare cancer], and while I don't know if it motivates me, it certainly doesn't allow for those little things that happen in life to worry me. I find I just get on with business and play the game I love.

How important is living in the 'now' when you're playing?

In terms of T20 it's crucial. You can't afford to get too flustered or read too much into what may have just happened, because the game goes so fast. If you're two overs behind the game, it can cost your team the match. You need to deal with whatever has happened there and then, move forward and make the next best decision. That's why it's important to have a clear mind.

What's your personal motto?

For T20 it's to enjoy the moment and don't play scared: keep a clear mind and play what's in front of you.

REMEMBER TO BREATHE

CHRIS GREEN

SYDNEY THUNDER
All-rounder

Getty Images

Describe your role in the Sydney Thunder.

In a nutshell I'm the second spin bowler to Fawad Ahmed, and offer some extra lower-order hitting and to try to get to the 'hot spots' in the field.

How do you cope with the pressure of a BBL match?

We did a really good breathing exercise before BBL|04. We sat on the bottom of a pool (and for safety reasons you shouldn't do this on your own, we actually had lifesavers on standby) to become aware of our breathing and finding our 'happy space' so we could perform at our best under pressure. That's helped me when a situation became tense, like when I bowled the 17th over in the BBL final. I take a deep breath before each ball whether I'm batting, bowling or fielding, to try and level down and concentrate on the skill that's required.

Describe your approach to training.

Our coach Paddy Upton advised me I'm the person who knows my body best and what it requires. There are days when you might need to train flat out for three or four hours and the next day you might only need a 20-minute top-up. You can't take away from the team environment, but it's important to know how best to prepare yourself for game day.

Who have you learnt the most from?

We were fortunate at the Thunder to have the big four: Mike Hussey, Jacques Kallis, Shane Watson and Andre Russell. They always made time to chat. I spent a lot of time talking to Huss and Watto about my game. I realised the reason they've succeeded is because they're genuine to who they are. They know what's made them successful and stay true to that.

Is there a story that inspires you?

As a boy growing up in South Africa I idolised Jacques Kallis, and to play alongside him at the Thunder was incredible. I like the way he goes about things—there's no fuss. He went through some tough times in South Africa; he carried the team for a long time and I liked that he never commented on it publicly. That was inspiring, and I'm trying to follow in his footsteps—as tough as that is.

What's your personal motto?

My dad's best friend said to me: 'Life is not a race, it's a journey.' I've taken that to mean to enjoy each day and to be a better person with it.

TEAMS

ADELAIDE Strikers

FOUNDED:	2011
COLOUR:	Blue
HOME GROUND:	Adelaide Oval
TITLES:	None
HIGHEST ALL-TIME RUN-SCORER:	Tim Ludeman 778
HIGHEST ALL-TIME WICKET-TAKER:	Kane Richardson 35
MOST CATCHES:	Tim Ludeman 20
GAME RESULTS BBL|05:	**Wins:** 7 • **Losses:** 1
POSITION FINISHED BBL|05:	Lost semi final; finished regular season first
BIGGEST BBL|05 HOME CROWD:	49,115 v Hobart Hurricanes, Adelaide Oval (13 January 2016)
MOST BBL|05 RUNS:	Travis Head 299 **HS:** 101* • **Av:** 42.71 • **S/R:** 154.92
MOST BBL|05 WICKETS:	Adil Rashid 16 **BBI:** 3–23 • **Av:** 14.12 • **Econ:** 6.51 • **S/R:** 13
MOST BBL|05 CATCHES:	Tim Ludeman/Travis Head 5
BBL|05 SQUAD:	Brad Hodge (c), Jono Dean, Travis Head, Jon Holland, Mahela Jayawardene, Alex Keath, Hamish Kingston, Ben Laughlin, Jake Lehmann, Tim Ludeman, Michael Neser, Gary Putland, Adil Rashid, Kane Richardson, Alex Ross, Craig Simmons, Kelvin Smith, Billy Stanlake, Greg West **Coach:** Jason Gillespie
PLAYER OF THE YEAR:	Adil Rashid

Strikers strike: Adelaide celebrates the dismissal of Tom Cooper in their match against the Melbourne Renegades at Etihad Stadium.

SEASON SNAPSHOT BBL|05

The Strikers had plenty of highlights during BBL|05: Travis Head's breathtaking innings to win what seemed an unwinnable match against the Sixers; Jake Lehmann's big six off the final ball to beat the Hurricanes; a classic catch to Alex Ross. But they again stumbled at the final hurdle and missed out on a place in the Big Final when they lost their semi final to the Sydney Thunder in front of a partisan home crowd. The Strikers, who lost only two games during the tournament—both to the Thunder—suffered a setback one month before their first game when West Indies power hitter Kieron Pollard was ruled out of action because of a knee injury. Despite the disappointing outcome, coach Jason Gillespie took heart from knowing that when his team found itself in trouble someone always stood up to be counted—such as Head against the Sixers.

PLAYER'S VERDICT

Adelaide's wicketkeeper-batsman Tim Ludeman knows the Strikers' huge crowds want more consistency from their team.

Adelaide suffered a semi-final loss for a second straight year. What needs to be done to go that extra step?

I think we need to be more consistent across the board in BBL|06, and hopefully deliver on the big stage when it matters most. Playing in front of 50,000 people every game prepares you for that, but unfortunately we've slipped at the key moment for the last two seasons.

What lessons have the Strikers taken from BBL|05?

We were unlucky with Kieron Pollard going down at the start of the tournament, but in saying that we secured a fantastic replacement in Mahela Jayawardene. We had a new coach in Jason 'Dizzy' Gillespie, and we had another new addition from England in Adil Rashid. And while it took a little while to get used to them, they fitted in brilliantly as people. Now we've had a whole season together it ought to hold us in good stead in gelling and making that final we're all striving for.

Describe Jason Gillespie as a coach.

He's fantastic. He obviously brings a wealth of knowledge from his playing days, and his coaching record speaks for itself. I know the younger players—guys like Travis Head and Jake Lehmann—have flourished under him.

Name Adelaide's best player in BBL|05.

I'd say Adil Rashid just pipped Travis Head. Rashid was very impressive and a lot of batters struggled to pick him. His bowling was unbelievable and he came through with the bat on a couple of occasions to help get us out of trouble. While I've nominated Rashid, Travis Head was brilliant.

What was your magic moment from BBL|05?

Travis Head's century on New Year's Eve; you couldn't have scripted that any better. He struck the ball so cleanly on a night when no one else could. It was exceptional.

PREVIEW OF BBL|06

THE DRAW

V BRISBANE HEAT
Adelaide Oval,
21 December 2016

V PERTH SCORCHERS
#TheFurnace,
23 December 2016

V SYDNEY SIXERS
Adelaide Oval,
31 December 2016

V HOBART HURRICANES
Blundstone Arena,
2 January 2017

V HOBART HURRICANES
Adelaide Oval,
6 January 2017

V MELBOURNE STARS
MCG, 10 January 2017

V MELBOURNE RENEGADES
Adelaide Oval,
16 January 2017

V SYDNEY THUNDER
Spotless Stadium,
18 January 2017

BBL|06 SQUAD

Jonathan Dean, Travis Head, Brad Hodge, Jon Holland, Hamish Kingston, Ben Laughlin, Jake Lehmann, Tim Ludeman, Michael Neser, Kieron Pollard, Adil Rashid, Kane Richardson, Craig Simmons, Kelvin Smith, Billy Stanlake **Coach:** Jason Gillespie

THREE KEY PLAYERS

MICHAEL NESER

The South African–born all-rounder, who emigrated to the Gold Coast with his family when he was 10, has excited plenty of people with his ability to bowl around the 150 km/h mark and average 20 with the bat in each of cricket's three formats. Although injuries hampered the early stages of the 26-year-old's career, Neser was picked for the 2014 Australia A team that played the Proteas in a four-dayer. He gave an insight into his potency in BBL|03 when he was named Adelaide's most valuable player.

JON HOLLAND

This naturally attacking spinner proved his calibre as a bowler during the 2015 Matador Cup competition when he took 14 wickets for Victoria at an average of 17.86. Holland was identified early in his career as a player of immense promise, hurtling through the ranks to be named in the Australian 15-man squad that toured India in 2009 for a seven-match one-day international series just 12 months after making his state debut. While his career has been frustrated by a series of shoulder injuries, Holland prides himself on making the ball drift in the air.

KIERON POLLARD

The powerful West Indian was forced out of BBL|05 four weeks before the opening match against the Melbourne Stars when he injured his knee while playing in South Africa's domestic T20 competition—and it proved a massive blow for the Strikers. Jason Gillespie's team missed his authority, and ended the season falling one win short of qualifying for the final. While Pollard made only 28 runs in the four matches he played in BBL|04 he provided a glimpse of his potential in a practice match, when he blasted Jon Holland's first five balls for six at Prince Alfred College.

ADELAIDE Strikers

Power 'n' passion: West Indies import Kieron Pollard blasts a big six for Adelaide during BBL|04. He'll add some explosiveness to the Strikers' batting order.

Pace ace: South African-born but Gold Coast raised Michael Neser excites plenty of people with his ability to unleash 150 km/h fireballs at will.

Natural attacker: Jon Holland was rewarded with tremendous form during 2015–16 by being rushed over to Sri Lanka as a member of Australia's Test team.

WHAT'S IN STORE FOR THIS SEASON

BEST-CASE SCENARIO

That Adelaide carries the momentum they displayed throughout most of BBL|05 into the finals series. The Strikers dominated last summer but slipped up in their home semi final against the Sydney Thunder. It was a bad blow for Jason Gillespie's team, but if they could carry that momentum through to the final anything would be possible because the Strikers boast some of the competition's best young talent.

BIGGEST CHALLENGE

Adelaide's biggest challenge is to continue with that momentum they've had over the past few years by way of home-ground advantage and a fanatical supporter base. They need to ensure they somehow get into that final four, but one challenge for them will be to actually not think about making the final . . . if they start the season with that on their minds it'll be a tough job to get there.

Adam Gilchrist

GILCHRIST GOLD

MY KEY PLAYER: Englishman Adil Rashid was brilliant for Adelaide last season but Travis Head is their key player. After admitting he started BBL|05 slowly he unleashed—and how—and we gained a tremendous insight into what a talented 22-year-old with no fear is capable of. I'm looking forward to seeing him build on last summer's spectacular performances.

BRISBANE HEAT

FOUNDED:	2011
COLOUR:	Teal
HOME GROUND:	The Gabba, Brisbane
TITLES:	One—BBL|02
HIGHEST ALL-TIME RUN-SCORER:	Chris Lynn 1103
HIGHEST ALL-TIME WICKET-TAKER:	Ben Cutting 26
MOST CATCHES:	Peter Forrest 15
GAME RESULTS BBL|05:	**Wins:** 3 • **Losses:** 5
POSITION FINISHED BBL|05:	Sixth
BIGGEST BBL|05 HOME CROWD:	33,783 v Adelaide Strikers, The Gabba (8 January 2016)
MOST BBL|05 RUNS:	Chris Lynn 378 **HS:** 101 • **Av:** 54 • **S/R:** 173.39
MOST BBL|05 WICKETS:	Samuel Badree 9 **BBI:** 5–22 • **Av:** 22.66 • **Econ:** 6.37 • **S/R:** 21.3
MOST BBL|05 CATCHES:	Lendl Simmons 5
BBL|05 SQUAD:	Chris Lynn (c), Samuel Badree, Nick Buchanan, Joe Burns, Ben Cutting, Alex Doolan, Andrew Fekete, Luke Feldman, Jason Floros, Peter Forrest, Sam Heazlett, James Hopes, Josh Lalor, James Peirson, Nathan Reardon, Lendl Simmons, Mark Steketee, Mitchell Swepson, Jack Wildermuth **Coach:** Daniel Vettori
PLAYER OF THE YEAR:	Chris Lynn

Dizzy dangerman: Samuel Badree, one of T20 cricket's most effective bowlers, celebrates the dismissal of Melbourne Stars batter Rob Quiney at the MCG.

SEASON SNAPSHOT BBL|05

Brisbane underwent massive changes after finishing last on the BBL|04 ladder by appointing former New Zealand international Daniel Vettori as their new coach. While they started their campaign sluggishly with a seven-wicket loss to the Renegades, two defeats to Hobart and then Perth, the Chris Lynn-captained Heat rallied in the second-half of the league, winning three matches only to fall painfully short of a semi final spot. While Lynn was outstanding—his haul of 378 runs included 27 sixes—it felt as though the BBL finished just as Brisbane was heating up. While they found their groove a game too late, their performances suggested they have the man-power needed to win a tournament. West Indian import Samuel Badree used his time in Queensland to enhance his reputation as one of the world's best T20 bowlers. His five-wicket effort in the shock victory over the Stars at the MCG was a definite season highlight.

PLAYER'S VERDICT

Joe Burns, a member of the Brisbane Heat, remembers BBL|05 as the season that proved the potential within his team's ranks.

What were the messages in Brisbane's season debrief?

Even though we came sixth there were good signs, because by the end of the tournament we'd found a style of play that really suits us. We relied heavily upon Chris Lynn but by our last game we'd settled our combinations and I think, had we cracked the top four, we would have been a real chance of winning the title.

What areas will the Heat be wanting to improve in for BBL|05?

Our batting has actually been a strength of ours for a long time. We have some very talented and skilful bowlers, but it's just a matter of trying to put those assets into one team. I think we sorted that out by the end of the tournament, and that's why BBL|06 is so exciting for us.

Who was Brisbane's most valuable player?

Chris Lynn. His batting was phenomenal but his captaincy was exceptional. He led on and off the field, and that was huge for us. He'll continue growing, and while we have [former New Zealand skipper] Brendon McCullum joining us for BBL|06 and it seems as though he'll captain us, it's really crucial that we also have a homegrown leader like Lynny in our ranks.

Can you pinpoint your magic moment from BBL|05?

The power hitting that was displayed in our game against the Hobart Hurricanes at the Gabba was incredible. Daniel Christian was hitting big sixes out of the stadium for Hobart, but when Chris Lynn came into bat for us it was as though he went toe to toe with Dan, hitting balls into the upper deck of the stands as well. It was amazing to watch such a big-hitting display.

THE DRAW

V ADELAIDE STRIKERS
Adelaide Oval,
21 December 2016

V SYDNEY THUNDER
Spotless Stadium,
28 December 2016

V HOBART HURRICANES
The Gabba,
30 December 2016

V SYDNEY SIXERS
The Gabba,
3 January 2017

V PERTH SCORCHERS
#TheFurnace,
5 January 2017

V PERTH SCORCHERS
The Gabba,
11 January 2017

V MELBOURNE STARS
MCG, 17 January 2017

V MELBOURNE RENEGADES
The Gabba,
20 January 2017

BBL|06 SQUAD

Samuel Badree, Joe Burns, Ben Cutting, Alex Doolan, Andrew Fekete, Luke Feldman, Jason Floros, Sam Heazlett, Josh Lalor, Chris Lynn, Brendon McCullum, James Peirson, Nathan Reardon, Alex Ross, Mark Steketee, Mitchell Swepson, Jack Wildermuth **Coach:** Daniel Vettori

PREVIEW OF BBL|06

THREE KEY PLAYERS

BRENDON McCULLUM

New Zealand cricket's loss is definitely the Brisbane Heat's gain with the Black Caps' former captain signed to add his authority to a team that has endured two disappointing seasons. McCullum played for the Heat in BBL|01—his nose was cracked by a 140 km/h Brett Lee delivery in the team's first-ever game—and he returns as one of world cricket's most respected leaders after helping orchestrate the Kiwis' charge to the 2015 World Cup final. He's regarded as one of the best strikers of the ball and has been described as 'brash, brutal and brilliant' to watch.

ALEX ROSS

Alex Ross joins the Heat from the Adelaide Strikers as the reigning Bradman Young Cricketer of the Year, and he's expected to galvanise Brisbane's middle order. Born in Melbourne but raised in Christchurch, where his father Ashley was New Zealand's assistant coach, he was christened 'The Sweepologist' by Network Ten commentator Damien Fleming because of his penchant for the shot, a legacy from his hockey days. Coach Daniel Vettori targeted him as a must-have recruit because he believes playing in the Heat's teal battle colours will enhance the 24-year-old's game. He's a handy fielder, taking a screamer in the outfield for Adelaide during the tense New Year's Eve match against the Sydney Sixers.

MARK STEKETEE

The Steketee–Fekete bowling combination formed a challenging tongue twister for the commentators during BBL|05, but they'd better master it quickly, because this 22-year-old from the Queensland country town of Warwick is viewed by the club's inner sanctum as a long-term prospect. When he debuted for the Heat in BBL|02, Steketee made the two-hour drive to the Big Smoke to train and play in matches. His T20 career started off on a positive note when he took a wicket in his first over for the Heat. He's determined to build on the four matches he played last summer.

WHAT'S IN STORE FOR THIS SEASON

BEST-CASE SCENARIO

That they get into the semis. They haven't finished in the top four since BBL|02 when they won the title, but to do that they'll need to get out of the blocks with some early victories. That would also generate plenty of enthusiasm from their supporters and that would, in turn, make the Gabba an uninviting place for visiting teams. We saw Brisbane start to gel towards the end of last summer and they looked a very dangerous outfit.

BIGGEST CHALLENGE

That the Brisbane Heat can provide some support around Chris Lynn out in the middle. Lynn was BBL|05's King of the Six with 27 sixers but he was also a lone wolf last summer. Perhaps their season might've had a different ending had one or two players provided him with more back-up. The arrival of former New Zealand captain Brendon McCullum is significant because he could be the support act Lynn needs.

Adam Gilchrist

Outback express: Fast bowler Mark Steketee continues to make massive inroads for the Heat since being recruited from Queensland country.

BRISBANE HEAT

Super standards: Powerful batter Brendon McCullum joins Brisbane Heat and is regarded by many as one of the great leaders in world cricket.

BBL belter: Test great Adam Gilchrist believes the Brisbane Heat's top order must provide run-scoring machine Chris Lynn with much greater support during BBL|06.

GILCHRIST GOLD

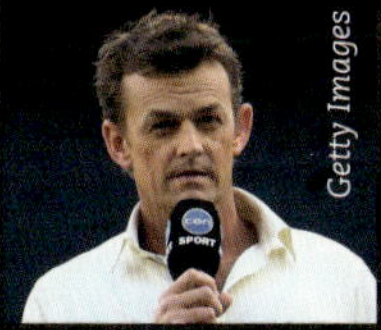

MY KEY PLAYER: Brendon McCullum, a foundation player for the Heat, returns as one of world cricket's most respected leaders. He'll add plenty of authority to the Daniel Vettori-coached team but as an experienced T20 player he offers an explosive batting style. His effort to strike the fastest century in Test history highlights his potency.

FOUNDED:	2011
COLOUR:	Purple
HOME GROUND:	Blundstone Arena, Hobart
TITLES:	None
HIGHEST ALL-TIME RUN-SCORER:	Tim Paine 883
HIGHEST ALL-TIME WICKET-TAKER:	Ben Laughlin 35
MOST CATCHES:	George Bailey 15
GAME RESULTS BBL|05:	**Wins:** 3 • **Losses:** 5
POSITION FINISHED BBL|05:	Seventh
BIGGEST BBL|05 HOME CROWD:	18,149 v Perth Scorchers, Blundstone Arena (10 January 2016)
MOST BBL|05 RUNS:	George Bailey 240 **HS:** 62* • **Av:** 60 • **S/R:** 150
MOST BBL|05 WICKETS:	Cameron Boyce 11 **BBI:** 3–34 • **Av:** 22.09 • **Econ:** 8.37 • **S/R:** 15.8
MOST BBL|05 CATCHES:	Tim Paine 8
BBL|05 SQUAD:	Tim Paine (c), George Bailey, Cameron Boyce, Daniel Christian, Ben Dunk, Michael Hill, Joe Mennie, Dom Michael, Simon Milenko, Sam Rainbird, Jake Reed, Clive Rose, Darren Sammy, Kumar Sangakkara, Shaun Tait, Timm van der Gugten, Beau Webster, Jonathan Wells **Coach:** Damien Wright
PLAYER OF THE YEAR:	Daniel Christian

Flashes of brilliance: Plenty of high fives after Perth dangerman Adam Voges was dismissed at Blundstone Arena.

SEASON SNAPSHOT BBL|05

Hobart showed flashes of brilliance throughout BBL|05: their 11-run victory over the competition's eventual winners, the Thunder, provided a frustrating glimpse of their true potential. While the form of then 32-year-old pace bowler Shaun Tait earned him a recall to Australia's T20 team, and leg spinner Cameron Boyce proved his class against the league's best, Hobart paid for its poor batting.

That was no better reflected than at the halfway mark of the tournament, when statistics highlighted that the Hurricanes had failed to make any headway in the powerplay. Coach Damien Wright warned his team that their record for worst net run rate in the competition would bruise their finals aspirations. At that stage, with three games remaining, it was –1.057.

While the average number of runs scored by all teams during a BBL|05 powerplay when Wright raised his concern was 43.7, the Hurricanes averaged 35.2. Unfortunately, it summed up the story of their summer of discontent.

PLAYER'S VERDICT

The Hurricanes' leg spinner Cameron Boyce looks back on a season when a Sri Lankan great made his presence felt in Hobart.

How badly did the last-ball loss to Adelaide—when Jake Lehmann hit a six—hurt Hobart's season?

It's easy to say that match cost us a finals berth, but we had losses earlier in the season that were critical. We played a few poor games early on, and it took a while for us to get momentum.

What lessons did the Hurricanes take from BBL|05?

We need to ensure the whole team is contributing in as many games as possible. The entire Adelaide team performed very well throughout the tournament, and you could also say that about the Stars. We'll look to improve on that.

How did Kumar Sangakkara help the Hurricanes?

His experience was invaluable. Kumar is a professional: he does all the little things very well and he was happy to talk to anyone, and he offered to help them whenever they needed it. Kumar said he wished he performed better, but for someone of his stature there's always so much expectation, although our coach Damien Wright didn't put that on him. Even if he didn't play, it's wonderful just to have Kumar Sangakkara around.

What was your BBL|05 highlight?

I enjoyed that I bowled against all of the big-name players. I like to put my hand up and put myself in those situations because that's when you get tested. This is my third year [in the BBL] and I've managed to take over 10 wickets each year. I take pride in that because it's very hard to be consistent in the BBL.

Name the Hurricanes' best player in BBL|05

Kumar Sangakkara. What he brought to the team was invaluable. It ranged from helping the boys at training to offering great advice on the field when we were under the pump.

THE DRAW

V SYDNEY SIXERS
SCG, 23 December 2016

V MELBOURNE STARS
Blundstone Arena,
26 December 2016

V BRISBANE HEAT
The Gabba,
30 December 2016

V ADELAIDE STRIKERS
Blundstone Arena,
2 January 2017

V ADELAIDE STRIKERS
Adelaide Oval,
6 January 2017

V SYDNEY THUNDER
Blundstone Arena,
8 January 2017

V MELBOURNE RENEGADES
Etihad Stadium,
12 January 2017

V PERTH SCORCHERS
Blundstone Arena,
21 January 2017

BBL|06 SQUAD

George Bailey, Cameron Boyce, Stuart Broad, Dan Christian, Ben Dunk, Ben McDermott, Dom Michael, Simon Milenko, Tim Paine, Sam Rainbird, Jake Reed, Clive Rose, Kumar Sangakkara, Shaun Tait, Jonathan Wells
Coach: Damien Wright

PREVIEW OF BBL|06

THREE KEY PLAYERS

TIM PAINE

Tim Paine created history in 2001 when, at just 16 years of age, he became the youngest player in Australia to be offered a first-class contract. Paine, who received a pair of batting pads from his grandmother for his second birthday, was earmarked as a future Test player from a young age. His international career was hampered by the recurrence of a serious finger injury, however after finishing BBL|05 with 239 runs, eight catches and a stumping, Paine re-enforced his value to the Hurricanes.

STUART BROAD

Hobart's BBL|06 campaign received a mighty boost when they recruited England fast bowler Stuart Broad, one of cricket's most competitive characters. Broad, who has taken 65 wickets in his 56 T20 internationals, is expected to add an extra dimension to a Hurricanes pace attack that already packed a powerful punch via Shaun Tait, Jack Reed and Sam Rainbird. Broad's presence adds extra lustre to a BBL franchise which boasts one of cricket's biggest names in Kumar Sangakkara. The ICC's No. 4 ranked Test bowler will be determined to make an impression; he wants his time at Hobart to help force his return to England's one-day international team.

SIMON MILENKO

A conservative number-cruncher by day, a dynamic run-getter and wicket-taker by night, Simon Milenko is a qualified accountant with a penchant for hitting the ball hard and tying up opposition batters with his medium-pace bowling. Milenko was given a taste of BBL during 2014–15 with the Brisbane Heat, and he did enough to impress Hobart's coaching staff. A proud product of Lismore in northern New South Wales, Milenko showcased his skills in the Hurricanes' first intra-squad trial when Sri Lankan great Kumar Sangakkara was among his four victims. He was impressive in his only BBL match, taking 3–25 against Adelaide.

Broad appeal: Stuart Broad will use his stint with the Hobart Hurricanes to try to force his way back into England's limited-overs teams.

WHAT'S IN STORE FOR THIS SEASON

BEST-CASE SCENARIO

That they're consistent in their regular season performances and lift for the run home to the semis. The Hurricanes have some great players on their roster with Kumar Sangakkara, George Bailey, Tim Paine, Shaun Tait, Dan Christian and Cameron Boyce among the best in the business; however, their win-loss pattern during BBL|05 would've frustrated their supporters. If they can string their wins together and constantly build momentum they could secure a semis berth.

BIGGEST CHALLENGE

Based on last season's performances it's going to be consistency. The Hurricanes haven't had consistent big strike rates—and partnerships—at the top of their order since Ben Dunk dominated BBL|03 with 395 runs. Hobart finished runners-up to Perth that season and there's no doubt their coach Damien Wright will be demanding for his players to tap back into what made them a force in 2013–14.

Adam Gilchrist

Paine and gain: Hobart's skipper Tim Paine led by example throughout a frustrating season for the Hurricanes.

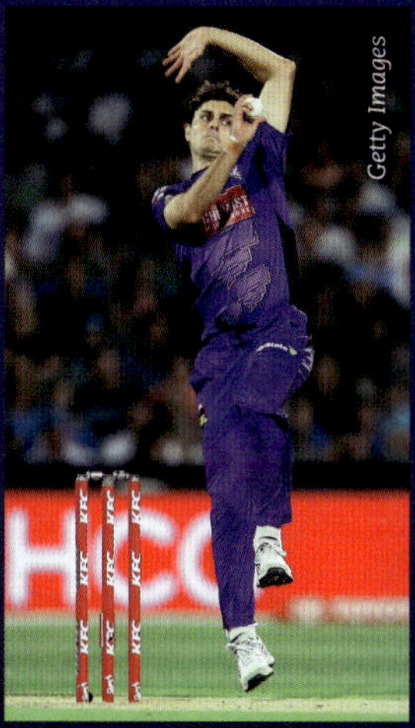

Number cruncher: Simon Milenko is a qualified accountant who likes to hammer the ball and tie up opposing batters with his medium-pace bowling.

GILCHRIST GOLD

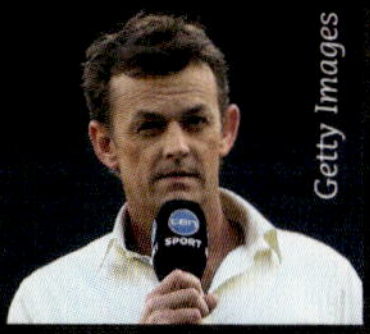

MY KEY PLAYER: Kumar Sangakkara and Dan Christian are two outstanding players, but Cameron Boyce impresses me as a leg spinner who is unafraid to take on the biggest names in the BBL. He finished last season with an impressive strike rate of 15.8 and he'll play an important hand in how the Hurricanes fare this season.

MELBOURNE RENEGADES

FOUNDED:	2011
COLOUR:	Red
HOME GROUND:	Etihad Stadium, Melbourne
TITLES:	None
HIGHEST ALL-TIME RUN-SCORER:	Aaron Finch 1207
HIGHEST ALL-TIME WICKET-TAKER:	Nathan Rimmington 30
MOST CATCHES:	Tom Cooper 16
GAME RESULTS BBL|05:	**Wins:** 3 • **Losses:** 5
POSITION FINISHED BBL|05:	Fifth
BIGGEST BBL|05 HOME CROWD:	43,176 v Melbourne Stars, Etihad Stadium (9 January 2016)
MOST BBL|05 RUNS:	Chris Gayle 260 **HS:** 56 • **Av:** 32.5 • **S/R:** 155.68
MOST BBL|05 WICKETS:	Nathan Rimmington 7 **BBI:** 4–26 • **Av:** 32.14 • **Econ:** 8.33 • **S/R:** 23.1
MOST BBL|05 CATCHES:	Tom Cooper 5
BBL|05 SQUAD:	Aaron Finch (c), Tom Beaton, Dwayne Bravo, Tom Cooper, Xavier Doherty, Callum Ferguson, Cameron Gannon, Chris Gayle, Nathan Hauritz, Ben McDermott, Peter Nevill, James Pattinson, Nathan Rimmington, Matthew Short, Peter Siddle, Cameron Stevenson, Chris Tremain, Matthew Wade, Guy Walker, Cameron White, Nick Winter **Coach:** David Saker
PLAYER OF THE YEAR:	Dwayne Bravo

High five: Chris Gayle and Xavier Doherty celebrate their combining to send Adelaide opener Tim Ludeman packing at Etihad Stadium.

SEASON SNAPSHOT BBL|05

The Renegades again boasted one of the best rosters in the BBL with Aaron Finch, Chris Gayle, Cameron White, Dwayne Bravo, Xavier Doherty, Peter Siddle, James Pattinson, Matthew Wade and Peter Nevill on their books. However, despite boasting genuine firepower, they finished in fifth place. Adding to their frustrations was being in positions to win some games but they failed to land the KO blow. Their loss to Perth at Etihad Stadium summed up their season. After being set a competitive 4–170, Michael Klinger and Shaun Marsh came out and steered the Scorchers to a 10-wicket victory. Finch was his team's rock and he received some support from Gayle—who, in the match against the Strikers, needed only 12 balls to score a world record equalling half century—and Bravo. Chris Tremain was rewarded for shouldering the bulk of his team's fast bowling responsibilities with selection in Australia A during the winter.

PLAYER'S VERDICT

Melbourne Renegades all-rounder Cameron White admitted that he and his teammates will be determined to do a better job of defending their totals in BBL|06.

What lessons did the Melbourne Renegades learn from BBL|05?

That we need to bowl and field a bit better. It's not only in the Big Bash, but in all the other T20 tournaments around the world the teams with the best bowling attacks do well.

What will the Renegades target in the lead-up to BBL|06?

You'll have to check in with the coaches, but everyone's game plan is pretty similar throughout the Big Bash; everyone talks about execution, so I have no doubt we'll be working on that. We'll also be looking at the areas we can improve on, look at the things that we didn't do so well in BBL|05.

Chris Gayle's 50 off 12 balls was a highlight. What does that kind of innings do for a team?

Chris seems to be able to do it consistently, so he's obviously very good at it. What it does for you, regardless of whether you're batting first or chasing a target, it sets the game up for you.

What was your magic moment from BBL|05?

We had a couple of great run chases that were pretty good. From a team point of view, we only won a few games, but the games we did win were enjoyable to play in.

It must have been tough to take when the Perth Scorchers' openers, Shaun Marsh and Michael Klinger, were sent in to chase a competitive 171 and they ran it down?

We posted some good scores but at times we couldn't defend them. The coaching staff and the players will be keen to rectify that.

Who was the Renegades' best player throughout BBL|05?

Aaron Finch only played five games for us, but he was well on his way to being our best player. However, Dwayne Bravo was our best player, and his form was rewarded by being named in the BBL|05 team of the tournament.

THE DRAW

V SYDNEY THUNDER
Etihad Stadium,
22 December 2016

V PERTH SCORCHERS
Etihad Stadium,
29 December 2016

V MELBOURNE STARS
MCG, 1 January 2017

V MELBOURNE STARS
Etihad Stadium,
7 January 2017

V SYDNEY SIXERS
SCG, 9 January 2017

V HOBART HURRICANES
Etihad Stadium,
12 January 2017

V ADELAIDE STRIKERS
Adelaide Oval,
16 January 2017

V BRISBANE HEAT
The Gabba,
20 January 2017

BBL|06 SQUAD

Tom Beaton, Dwayne Bravo, Tom Cooper, Xavier Doherty, Callum Ferguson, Aaron Finch, Marcus Harris, Brad Hogg, James Pattinson, Nathan Rimmington, Peter Siddle, Chris Tremain, Matthew Wade, Guy Walker, Cameron White, Nick Winter **Coach:** Andrew McDonald

PREVIEW OF BBL|06

THREE KEY PLAYERS

CALLUM FERGUSON

Callum Ferguson's BBL|05 campaign was cruelled by the ACL tear he suffered in his left knee while fielding in an intra-squad trial match. It was a bitter blow for the 32-year-old after he started the season in deft touch, scoring a career best 213 against Tasmania in the Sheffield Shield. Ferguson, who has represented Australia in the one-day international and T20 arenas, says his role in the Renegades is to be the 'link man', to ensure big hitters such as Aaron Finch can shine. After he won a South Australian junior state tennis championship, his father, Jim, a respected tennis coach, wanted him to hit the professional circuit, but cricket was Ferguson's passion.

DWAYNE BRAVO

All-rounder Dwayne Bravo reached record figures in the aftermath of the West Indies' World T20 triumph when his song 'Champion' went viral, with more than 17 million people watching the Trinidadian's music video on YouTube. Bravo, who took 6 wickets and scored 201 runs for the Renegades in BBL|05, said he had a gut feeling that the right time to release the song was just before the World Cup, and he credited the Windies success with catapulting it up the charts. He is a distant relative of Windies great Brian Lara, and says the master batsman's rise and rise inspired him to play.

AARON FINCH

Testimony to his determination, five weeks after Aaron Finch injured his left hamstring while racing through for a quick single in a one-day international against India he was in the thick of a T20 international against South Africa, hitting 40 off 18 deliveries. He used the 2016 Indian Premier League season to dismiss suggestions he struggles against spin by winning three man of the match awards in his opening five games for the Gujarat Lions. He blasted 246 runs for the Renegades in BBL|05 at an average of 49.20, becoming the first batter to crash through the BBL's 1000-run barrier when he scored 65 in the Renegades' victory over the Brisbane Heat.

WHAT'S IN STORE FOR THIS SEASON

BEST-CASE SCENARIO

That the Renegades are provided a true and consistent wicket at Etihad Stadium because the men in red have a strong bowling line-up with James Pattinson, Peter Siddle, Chris Tremain, Nathan Rimmington, Xavier Doherty and now Brad Hogg. They also boast a skilful batting line-up that blends explosive power with deft touch . . . all they need is for their wicket to not be the lottery it has been in recent seasons.

BIGGEST CHALLENGE

It's not a new one for the Renegades but they'll need to again fill the void when Aaron Finch and Matt Wade are invariably called up for international duties midway through the tournament. Finch scored 246 runs at 49.20 from five games last summer while wicketkeeper Wade hit 77 runs from 64 balls. They're important members of their team's batting line-up and during their absence individuals have to take responsibility and score their runs.

Adam Gilchrist

Back in business: Former Australian player Callum Ferguson is ready to roll after being sidelined for all of BBL|05 by a knee injury.

MELBOURNE RENEGADES

Bravo, Dwayne: West Indies star Dwayne Bravo seems as though he's ready for take-off after dismissing Marcus Stoinis in the derby.

Barrier breaker: T20 run-scoring machine Aaron Finch became the first player to smash through the BBL's 1000 run barrier during BBL|05.

GILCHRIST GOLD

MY KEY PLAYER: I really admire Cameron White because he has the tenacity and the desire to keep proving to people he can compete at this level. Whenever people write White off he consistently produces the goods to silence them and it pleases me no end to see he still possesses a fierce hunger to succeed.

FOUNDED:	2011
COLOUR:	Green
HOME GROUND:	Melbourne Cricket Ground
TITLES:	None
HIGHEST ALL-TIME RUN-SCORER:	Luke Wright 1136
HIGHEST ALL-TIME WICKET-TAKER:	John Hastings 40
MOST CATCHES:	Luke Wright 21
GAME RESULTS BBL|05:	**Wins:** 5 • **Losses:** 3
POSITION FINISHED BBL|05:	Runners-up; finished regular season second
BIGGEST BBL|05 HOME CROWD:	80,883 v Melbourne Renegades, Melbourne Cricket Ground (2 January 2016)
MOST BBL|05 RUNS:	Kevin Pietersen 323 **HS:** 76 • **Av:** 40.37 • **S/R:** 159.11
MOST BBL|05 WICKETS:	Adam Zampa 12 **BBI:** 2–16 • **Av:** 22.50 • **Econ:** 7.10 • **S/R:** 19
MOST BBL|05 CATCHES:	Peter Handscomb 10
BBL|05 SQUAD:	David Hussey (c), Michael Beer, Scott Boland, James Faulkner, Seb Gotch, Evan Gulbis, Peter Handscomb, Sam Harper, John Hastings, Ben Hilfenhaus, Glenn Maxwell, Kevin Pietersen, Rob Quiney, Marcus Stoinis, Tom Triffitt, Daniel Worrall, Luke Wright, Adam Zampa **Coach:** Stephen Fleming

Shining star: Marcus Stoinis is the centre of attention after he dismissed Perth's Ashton Turner at #TheFurnace in the run home to the finals.

SEASON SNAPSHOT BBL|05

The Melbourne Stars—who'd never progressed beyond the BBL's semi-final stage before BBL|05—enjoyed their best season by qualifying for the Big Final under their new coach, Stephen Fleming. They played the title decider without high-profile players John Hastings, Glenn Maxwell, Scott Boland and James Faulkner, who were called up for the one-day international series against India. Kevin Pietersen continued his princely form by blasting 74 from 64 deliveries to guide his team to a competitive 176. While there's certain to be a sense of 'unfinished business' after falling short, it was still a season for the Stars to savour. They hosted the league's record 80,883 crowd that attended the Melbourne derby; Pietersen smashed 323 runs from nine innings; coach Fleming and captain David Hussey provided strong leadership; leg-spinner Adam Zampa was a revelation; Luke Wright scored a magnificent century; while the likes of Daniel Worrall, Evan Gulbis and Marcus Stoinis provided depth—and a cutting edge.

PLAYER'S VERDICT

While the Melbourne Stars just missed out on winning the title, their captain, David Hussey, described BBL|05 as a breakthrough season.

Melbourne Stars broke through for their first taste of a Big Final. How did that feel?

It was more a relief than a sense of elation. It was a monkey off the back, and now we can move forward and just focus on winning the trophy.

You lost the final to the Thunder. What did you take from that game?

It was a great game of cricket to play in, and in front of our home fans. The result was disappointing but, to be fair, I thought both teams played a very even style of a game, but unfortunately we finished second in a few crucial moments. I think the final was a good advertisement for T20 cricket in this country, and hopefully we'll have a few more finals like that.

Your brother Mike retired after leading the Thunder to their title. Will you miss the rivalry you share?

No, not really! Mike has gone out a winner and deservedly so. He's been a great of the game, and hopefully he enjoys a lot of success in the future.

What was your magic moment from BBL|05?

Luke Wright's century against the Melbourne Renegades in front of 80,000 people at the MCG was special. It was the local derby and Luke was probably struggling for runs at that stage, and by his own admission he wanted to put on a big show and didn't he do that? It was a great innings to watch in front of a packed house. Such a big occasion.

Who do you think was the Stars' best player in BBL|05?

There was a lottery of four, with Scott Boland, John Hastings, Kevin Pietersen and Adam Zampa. They all played well, but the two stand-outs were Scott Boland and Kevin Pietersen. They were brilliant all summer.

PREVIEW OF BBL|06

THE DRAW

V HOBART HURRICANES
Blundstone Arena,
26 December 2016

V MELBOURNE RENEGADES
MCG, 1 January 2017

V SYDNEY THUNDER
Spotless Stadium,
4 January 2017

V MELBOURNE RENEGADES
Etihad Stadium,
7 January 2017

V ADELAIDE STRIKERS
MCG, 10 January 2017

V PERTH SCORCHERS
#TheFurnace,
14 January 2017

V BRISBANE HEAT
MCG, 17 January 2017

V SYDNEY SIXERS
MCG, 21 January 2017

BBL|06 SQUAD

David Hussey (c), Michael Beer, Scott Boland, James Faulkner, Sebastian Gotch, Evan Gulbis, Peter Handscomb, Sam Harper, John Hastings, Ben Hilfenhaus, Glenn Maxwell, Kevin Pietersen, Robert Quiney, Marcus Stoinis, Tom Triffitt, Daniel Worrall, Luke Wright, Adam Zampa
Coach: Stephen Fleming

THREE KEY PLAYERS

SCOTT BOLAND

Scott Boland transformed himself from a 'barrel-shaped' kid into an international-class fast bowler, replacing his injured Stars teammate John Hastings on the Australian team's recent tour of the West Indies. Boland, whose weight peaked at 118 kilograms, admitted he was embarrassed when playing for the 2010 Victorian Futures League team to see that many of the players who took their shirts off had six packs. He whittled his weight down to 96 kilograms by following a strict diet, and says he feels as though he's lost a 'bag of cement'. He now fields balls he once wouldn't have reached, and instead of running out of puff maintains his pace throughout a match.

JAMES FAULKNER

James Faulkner's ability to get his team home in tight run chases puts him in the same league as former Australian one-day international Michael Bevan. The 26-year-old's calmness under pressure has gained him a reputation as 'The Finisher'. Indeed, statisticians noted that in his first 35 one-day international innings, Faulkner hit the winning runs for Australia on nine occasions. While he took 6 wickets on his Test debut against England in 2013, he entered the record books for scoring the fastest century by an Australian one-day international player (since eclipsed by Glenn Maxwell), plundering 116 against India from only 57 deliveries in Bangalore.

EVAN GULBIS

Described as James Faulkner's 'apprentice' at Tasmania and then the Stars when he joined the green machine from the Hurricanes, the 30-year-old Gulbis was given an opportunity to perform in five matches during BBL|05. He finished the tournament as the star-studded outfit's surprise packet. Gulbis nailed 102 runs batting at No. 7, and his unconquered 61 against Brisbane was a genuine highlight. When Gulbis left Victoria to accept a Tasmanian Sheffield Shield berth he was regarded as a hard-hitting batter, but he evolved into an all-rounder thanks to his improved bowling. In 2013–14 he made the highest score by a No. 8 batsman in the Shield's history, hammering 229 against South Australia.

Peak condition: After working overtime on his fitness the Melbourne Stars' Scott Boland is one of the BBL's strike bowlers

WHAT'S IN STORE FOR THIS SEASON

BEST-CASE SCENARIO

It's to answer their critics and finally win the competition! The Stars have done everything possible to be a title-winning team; they've set solid foundations and last summer they added another floor to what they're building by qualifying for their inaugural final appearance. The Stars need BBL|06 to be the tournament in which they furnish the penthouse with the trophy. Until they do, it will be hard for them to sit back and savour what they've constructed.

BIGGEST CHALLENGE

The Stars had their roster finalised when their rivals were still recruiting players. That's going to be a huge plus for them because the players knew over the winter where they 'are'. The challenge before coach Stephen Fleming is to ensure every member of his squad is ready to excel at the final stage of the season because the Stars are certain to lose key players to international duties.

Adam Gilchrist

MELBOURNE STARS

Bevan connection: Melbourne Stars all-rounder James Faulkner has earned the reputation as the best finisher in limited overs cricket since Michael Bevan.

Opportunity knocked: All-rounder Evan Gulbis ensured he made the most of his chances with the start-studded Stars during BBL|05.

GILCHRIST GOLD

MY KEY PLAYER: I'm tipping Marcus Stoinis to have a bumper summer after showing glimpses of what he's capable of last season. He's being granted opportunities—such as playing for Australia A—and they're allowing him to grow as a cricketer. Those opportunities are also allowing for his confidence to grow—and that should pay dividends.

PERTH SCORCHERS

FOUNDED:	2011
COLOUR:	Orange
HOME GROUND:	#TheFurnace (the WACA Ground), Perth
TITLES:	Two—BBL|03 and BBL|04
HIGHEST ALL-TIME RUN-SCORER:	Shaun Marsh 1127
HIGHEST ALL-TIME WICKET-TAKER:	Brad Hogg 46
MOST CATCHES:	Adam Voges 22
GAME RESULTS BBL|05:	**Wins:** 5 • **Losses:** 3
POSITION FINISHED BBL|05:	Lost semi final; finished regular season third
BIGGEST BBL|05 HOME CROWD:	20,870 v Melbourne Stars, #TheFurnace (16 January 2016)
MOST BBL|05 RUNS:	Michael Klinger 285 **HS:** 90* • **Av:** 40.71 • **S/R:** 122.31
MOST BBL|05 WICKETS:	Andrew Tye 13 **BBI:** 3–22 • **Av:** 18 • **Econ:** 7.05 • **S/R:** 15.3
MOST BBL|05 CATCHES:	Cameron Bancroft 7
BBL|05 SQUAD:	Adam Voges (c), Ashton Agar, Cameron Bancroft, Jason Behrendorff, Michael Carberry, Nathan Coulter-Nile, Matt Dixon, Marcus Harris, Brad Hogg, Michael Klinger, Simon Mackin, Mitchell Marsh, Shaun Marsh, James Muirhead, Joel Paris, Ashton Turner, Andrew Tye, Sam Whiteman, David Willey **Coach:** Justin Langer
PLAYER OF THE YEAR:	David Willey

Perth & Paris: Scorchers fast bowler Joel Paris was ecstatic to have taken a catch off Jason Behrendorff's bowling to dismiss Adelaide's Tim Ludeman.

SEASON SNAPSHOT BBL|05

The Perth Scorchers are the BBL's most successful franchise, so every team lifts whenever they're pitted against them. This meant that the team coached by Justin Langer had a target on its back as it set its sights on a third consecutive title. The Scorchers' attack, however, maintained its reputation for strangling the life out of opposing line-ups, with Andrew Tye leading the charge. While Shaun Marsh was outstanding—averaging 72.66 from his five innings—unheralded English all-rounder David Willey made an indelible mark and was named player of the year. But the Scorchers suffered two unexpected back-to-back defeats to the Melbourne Stars, the most shattering when they needed to score only 109 to secure a home semi final but collapsed for 94. Langer attributed the shock result to his players being flat, but the loss of Nathan Coulter-Nile and Sam Whiteman to injuries, Jason Behrendorff's battle with a back problem, and the international commitments of Adam Voges and the Marsh brothers certainly took their toll.

PLAYER'S VERDICT

Perth Scorchers opener Shaun Marsh reflected on a summer upon which his team plans to build during BBL|06.

Many critics expected Perth to defend its BBL|04 title. Was that too much pressure?

Not at all, because we don't worry about what's being said about us. All we can control is what we do at training and on the pitch. We also realise it's important to stick together as a group. One of the great benefits from last summer is our young players now have a BBL season under their belt, and guys such as Cameron Bancroft and Joel Paris can take their games to another level in BBL|06.

Are rival teams starting to copy the Perth Scorchers' approach to T20?

I'm not too sure what other teams do, but we certainly work hard—especially during the Big Bash. I believe the guys get confidence going into big games knowing we've done the hard work off the field to give ourselves every chance to be at our best on game day. With that approach—and the squad we have—I'm certain we can go one step better than last summer, and that's to make the final and win it.

What did the Perth Scorchers gain from BBL|05?

After playing in the four previous Big Finals, it was obviously disappointing not to make it to a fifth one. Our biggest lesson came from those matches where we just didn't complete a full game. In T20, if you're off your game by five overs it's hard to win. While it was unfortunate to fall short, to qualify for another finals was special.

Name Perth's best player.

That's tough because we had so many good players. David Willey was outstanding; Michael Klinger never let us down; while some of our younger players such as Ashton Agar played beautifully. Cameron Bancroft showed what a great player he'll be; Joel Paris is one of the best young bowlers in Australia, and then there's A.J. Tye.

What was your magic BBL|05 moment?

The [opening 171-run] partnership 'Maxy' Klinger and I put on to beat the Melbourne Renegades. To win a game by 10 wickets is a special feeling—and to do it with a good mate added to the occasion.

PREVIEW OF BBL|06

THE DRAW

V ADELAIDE STRIKERS
#TheFurnace
23 December 2016

V SYDNEY SIXERS
SCG, 27 December 2016

V MELBOURNE RENEGADES
Etihad Stadium,
29 December 2016

V SYDNEY THUNDER
#TheFurnace,
1 January 2017

V BRISBANE HEAT
#TheFurnace,
5 January 2017

V BRISBANE HEAT
The Gabba,
11 January 2017

V MELBOURNE STARS
#The Furnace,
14 January 2017

V HOBART HURRICANES
Blundstone Arena,
21 January 2017

BBL|06 SQUAD

Ashton Agar, Cameron Bancroft, Jason Behrendorff, Hilton Cartwright, Nathan Coulter-Nile, Mitchell Johnson, Michael Klinger, Mitchell Marsh, Shaun Marsh, James Muirhead, Joel Paris, Jhye Richardson, Ashton Turner, Andrew Tye, Adam Voges, Sam Whiteman, David Willey **Coach:** Justin Langer

THREE KEY PLAYERS

CAMERON BANCROFT

As a youngster, Cameron Bancroft idolised Perth Scorchers coach Justin Langer, but he overcame his feelings of intimidation to approach 'J.L.' for advice, and the pair have since forged a positive relationship. Bancroft, now 24, has a Langer-like passion for cricket, and his improvement was acknowledged with selection for the doomed Test series against Bangladesh—doomed, because it was cancelled due to fears of a terrorist attack. Langer says Bancroft's work ethic separates him from other players. Bancroft, who can also keep, is expected to use BBL|06 as a platform to achieve his dream of wearing the baggy green Test cap.

ANDREW TYE

Andrew Tye—as in tying batsmen up—was selected in Australia's 2016 World T20 squad after he used BBL|05 to build his reputation as one of the league's best death bowlers. At the end of BBL|04, Australia's T20 skipper Aaron Finch described Tye as the 'find of the tournament', and his abilities earned him contracts in the Indian Premier League with the Chennai Super Kings and in England's T20 competition with Gloucestershire. He was a latecomer to elite cricket—Western Australia's selectors waited until he was 26 before unleashing him in the domestic one-day tournament. He didn't disappoint, finishing second in the wicket-taking tally.

MITCHELL JOHNSON

Mitchell Johnson will add to the Perth Scorchers pace attack after joining the BBL's two-time champions in 2016–17. Johnson will suit up for his first taste of the BBL's unique—and exciting—brand cricket after his international commitments prevented him from playing in the competition's first five seasons. Having retired from the Test team with 313 scalps, the 35-year-old will use his time at the Scorchers as his first step towards a coaching career by mentoring Perth's battalion of young pace aces. Johnson made it clear he still possesses the pace . . . and the menace . . . that made him one of the world's most feared fast bowlers: 'As soon as I get a sniff of the bounce, I get pretty fired up.'

PERTH SCORCHERS

WHAT'S IN STORE FOR THIS SEASON

BEST-CASE SCENARIO

That Mitchell Johnson comes into the Scorchers fully fresh, injury free and mad keen to give everything possible for the two-time BBL champions. After retiring from Test cricket with 313 wickets at an average of 28.40, Johnson will inject invaluable experience into Justin Langer's squad—and you'd imagine plenty of fear into rival batting line-ups. Perth's bowling attack has been outstanding since the BBL was formed, but Johnson has it in him to guide the likes of Joel Paris and Jason Behrendorff to reach even greater heights.

BIGGEST CHALLENGE

To replace Brad Hogg on the field—and off it—because 'Hoggy' enjoyed such a great cult following in Perth. He's an integral part of the history of the Scorchers and even at the grand old age of 44 he was still a quality performer. While Hoggy mightn't have taken the number of wickets he would've wanted last season—he finished with 6—his economy rate was an impressive 7.02. He'll be a big loss.

Adam Gilchrist

Bang-croft: Cameron Bancroft missed making his Test debut on the doomed tour of Bangladesh but he made an impact on BBL|05.

Tyed down: Perth's Andrew Tye maintained his reputation throughout BBL|05 as one of the league's best death bowlers.

Scorched Perth: Perth fans celebrated Mitchell Johnson's decision to play for the Scorchers after an outstanding career in Australia's green and gold battle colours.

GILCHRIST GOLD

MY KEY PLAYER: Mitchell Johnson, he's the prototype T20 bowler—he bowls fast, he can hit the ball hard while he's also athletic in the field. It also shapes as a new experience for Mitch because despite playing 112 T20 games and starring in the Indian Premier League he's never bowled in the BBL. I can't wait to see him steam in.

FOUNDED:	2011
COLOUR:	Magenta
HOME GROUND:	Sydney Cricket Ground
TITLES:	One—BBL|01
HIGHEST ALL-TIME RUN-SCORER:	Nic Maddinson 983
HIGHEST ALL-TIME WICKET-TAKER:	Brett Lee 35
MOST CATCHES:	Moises Henriques 17
GAME RESULTS BBL|05:	**Wins:** 2 • **Losses:** 6
POSITION FINISHED BBL|05:	Eighth
BIGGEST BBL|05 HOME CROWD:	38,456 v Sydney Thunder, Sydney Cricket Ground (16 January 2016)
MOST BBL|05 RUNS:	Michael Lumb 253 **HS:** 63 • **Av:** 31.62 • **S/R:** 133.15
MOST BBL|05 WICKETS:	Sean Abbott 11 **BBI:** 3/8 • **Av:** 19.54 • **Econ:** 10 • **S/R:** 11.7
MOST BBL|05 CATCHES:	Michael Lumb 5
BBL|05 SQUAD:	Moises Henriques (c), Nic Maddinson (c), Sean Abbott, Jackson Bird, Doug Bollinger, Johan Botha, Ryan Carters, Ed Cowan, Ben Dwarshuis, Brad Haddin, Trent Lawford, Michael Lumb, Nathan Lyon, Stephen O'Keefe, Jordan Silk, William Somerville **Coach:** Greg Shipperd
PLAYER OF THE YEAR:	Michael Lumb

Getty Images

Welcome respite: The Sixers savour a wicket during a season in which injuries and national team duty wasn't kind to their BBl|05 campaign.

SEASON SNAPSHOT BBL|05

The unavailability of numerous star players due to either injuries or national team duty had a disastrous impact on the Sixers' 2015–16 campaign, and contributed significantly to the team finishing BBL|05 with the wooden spoon. The recurrence of a calf problem for skipper Moises Henriques ended his season and struck at an unfortunate time. He was on 41 against the Melbourne Stars and was forced to hobble off, which probably denied his team a victory. BBL|05 will be remembered by the Sixers as a season of change, with former Stars mentor Greg Shipperd recruited to replace Trevor Bayliss, who had signed on to coach England's national teams. Brett Lee's retirement was also an important factor in how the season panned out for the men in magenta. While young gun Ben Dwarshuis won widespread praise for demanding the job of bowling the crucial final overs of an innings, the Sixers lacked Lee's knockout punch.

PLAYER'S VERDICT

Getty Images

The Sydney Sixers crashed from BBL|04 runners-up to wooden spooners and Stephen O'Keefe dissected a season that tested his team's depth.

It was a tough year for the Sixers. What happened?

There was a culmination of quite a few things: injuries to key players, we also had a changing of the guard in terms of the coaching structure, and Brett Lee's retirement was another factor. We had some new guys come in and we didn't adapt to change quickly enough and we were caught on the hop. The good news is we have the playing talent here, we just need to keep fit and be ready to go.

How will BBL|06 be different for the Sixers?

As a team that's used to winning, we're going to be hungry. We're determined to prove other people wrong. Finishing at the bottom of the table was embarrassing. We'll go back to basics, we'll build on the team culture and we'll translate that into results.

What was your highlight from BBL|05?

I'd say the turnaround of the Sydney Thunder. They copped a fair bit of stick over the years and I say full credit to Mike Hussey and [chief executive] Nick Cummins for turning that ship around. The Sixers' win over Hobart at the SCG was a highlight, and showed how we're able to play when we get everything right.

Who was your team's best player?

Michael Lumb was the deserved winner of our players' player—he had a couple of cracking innings. His effort in our win over the Melbourne Renegades was exceptional. Moises Henriques was on course to being our best player, but his season-ending calf injury cruelled that.

What's your advice to anyone who writes the Sixers off based on BBL|05?

Last year was a blip on the radar. We'll do what we've done in years gone by and just prove them wrong with our actions.

PREVIEW OF BBL|06

THE DRAW

V SYDNEY THUNDER
Spotless Stadium,
20 December 2016

V HOBART HURRICANES
SCG, 23 December 2016

V PERTH SCORCHERS
SCG, 27 December 2016

V ADELAIDE STRIKERS
Adelaide Oval,
31 December 2016

V BRISBANE HEAT
The Gabba,
3 January 2017

V MELBOURNE RENEGADES
SCG, 9 January 2017

V SYDNEY THUNDER
SCG, 14 January 2017

V MELBOURNE STARS
MCG, 21 January 2017

BBL|06 SQUAD

Sean Abbott, Jackson Bird, Doug Bollinger, Johan Botha, Ryan Carters, Ben Dwarshuis, Brad Haddin, Josh Hazlewood, Moises Henriques, Nathan Lyon, Nic Maddinson, Joe Mennie, Stephen O'Keefe, Jordan Silk, Mitchell Starc
Coach: Greg Shipperd

THREE KEY PLAYERS

BEN DWARSHUIS

This young fast bowler proved his mettle during BBL|05 when he volunteered to assume retired great Brett Lee's role of bowling the death overs at the end of an innings after the Sixers struggled to shut their opponents out. Dwarshuis accepted stand-in skipper Nic Maddinson's challenge to step up for what is a despair or glory job. The 22-year-old left-armer, who was compared to Mitchell Johnson when he burst onto the scene as an 18-year-old from Sydney's Sutherland club, showed plenty of promise in a tough season for the Sixers, his best effort 3–25 against the Adelaide Strikers.

MOISES HENRIQUES

After breaking his jaw in three places when he and Surrey teammate Rory Burns collided while attempting to take a catch in a T20 match in England, Moises Henriques' BBL|05 campaign lasted only three games due to the recurrence of a calf injury. He was on 41 and batting brilliantly against the Stars when he set off for a quick single and pulled up in agony. Henriques was picked in Australia A's team during the off-season, and the Sixers will be imploring Lady Luck to look more kindly upon him this summer. Apart from his obvious skills, the all-rounder's leadership is crucial.

BRAD HADDIN

Acknowledged as one of world cricket's fiercest competitors, Brad Haddin adds starch to any line-up. He's long been hailed as a player who leads by example; the former Australian wicketkeeper's ability to ignore the pain of the broken finger he took into a 2008 Test match against the West Indies provides a glimpse into his inner toughness. He's proud of his status as the Sixers' first signing so expect Haddin to demand a big improvement on the team's BBL|05 campaign.

Painful blow: Moises Henriques's leadership was sorely missed after he injured his troublesome calf muscle in the third game of the tournament.

Man of mettle: Fast bowler Ben Dwarshuis impressed plenty when he volunteered to take on the pressure of bowling at the death.

Don't play scared: Former Australian Test wicketkeeper Brad Haddin, regarded as one of cricket's fiercest competitors, provides the Sydney Sixers with plenty of authority.

WHAT'S IN STORE FOR THIS SEASON

BEST-CASE SCENARIO

That they get an early win over the Sydney Thunder. The Sixers won't want to let the Thunder's momentum following last season's title victory to carry through their city, and an early victory will make it easier for them to ensure that. After being the big brother for so long—they hadn't lost a game to their arch rivals until last season—the Sixers won't want to go from being the dominator to the dominated.

BIGGEST CHALLENGE

The Sixers were stunned to finish BBL|05 with the wooden spoon, but the test for them is to not overanalyse a season some players described as embarrassing. It's important the leadership team ensures the squad has a relaxed and fun environment to work in. If players such as Brad Haddin and Johan Botha—two players closer to the end of their careers than the beginning—are enjoying their cricket they'll contribute into their latter years.

Adam Gilchrist

GILCHRIST GOLD

MY KEY PLAYER: Nic Maddinson started last summer officially ranked the BBL's No. 1 batter, and while he mightn't have been overly happy with his campaign, the 24-year-old is an extraordinary talent. He craves consistency but there are plenty of supporters hoping he uses this summer to break through and make people take notice of him.

SYDNEY THUNDER

FOUNDED:	2011
COLOUR:	Lime Green
HOME GROUND:	Spotless Stadium, Sydney
TITLES:	One—BBL|05
HIGHEST ALL-TIME RUN-SCORER:	Usman Khawaja 819
HIGHEST ALL-TIME WICKET-TAKER:	Dirk Nannes 23
MOST CATCHES:	Ryan Carters 12
GAME RESULTS BBL|05:	**Wins:** 6 • **Losses:** 4
POSITION FINISHED BBL|05:	Champions; finished regular season fourth
BIGGEST BBL|05 HOME CROWD:	21,500 v Adelaide Strikers, Spotless Stadium (28 December 2015)
MOST BBL|05 RUNS:	Usman Khawaja 345 **HS:** 109* • **Av:** 172.50 • **S/R:** 163.50
MOST BBL|05 WICKETS:	Clint McKay 18 **BBI:** 4–28 • **Av:** 15.22 • **Econ:** 8.09 • **S/R:** 11.2
MOST BBL|05 CATCHES:	Chris Green 8
BBL|05 SQUAD:	Michael Hussey (c), Fawad Ahmed, Ahillen Beadle, Aiden Blizzard, Pat Cummins, Jake Doran, Ryan Gibson, Chris Green, Chris Hartley, Jacques Kallis, Usman Khawaja, Nathan McAndrew, Alistair McDermott, Andrew McDonald, Clint McKay, Henry Nicholls, Kurtis Patterson, Ben Rohrer, Andre Russell, Gurinder Sandhu, Shane Watson **Coach:** Paddy Upton
PLAYER OF THE YEAR:	Shane Watson and Usman Khawaja

Fairytale finish: Sydney Thunder celebrate their going from easybeats to world-beaters after winning the BBL|05 final at the MCG.

SEASON SNAPSHOT BBL|05

The Sydney Thunder's focused off-season recruitment drive lured Shane Watson, Andre Russell, Ben Rohrer and Clint McKay to join forces with Michael Hussey, Jacques Kallis and Usman Khawaja. While the team's average age was 33 years and 52 days, the experience ultimately provided the BBL's perennial battlers with a title-winning edge that erased four seasons of trials and tribulations. The Thunder started their campaign with a bang, recording their first-ever victory over arch rivals, the Sydney Sixers. The Paddy Upton-coached Thunder then proved their mettle by holding their nerve to defeat the star-studded Melbourne Stars by one heart-stopping run after Khawaja scored a majestic century. After being identified as title contenders, the 'jitters' threatened to undermine their season with four straight losses. However, they fought through to defeat Adelaide in the semi when Khawaja's second century of the tournament powered Sydney to an 8-wicket victory. With momentum in their favour, they defeated the Stars at the MCG to complete a BBL fairytale by being proclaimed champions.

PLAYER'S VERDICT

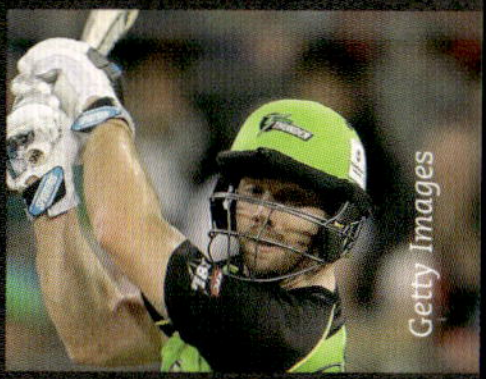

Sydney Thunder batsman Aiden Blizzard reflected on a season when his team transformed from easybeats into world-beaters.

What did we learn about the Sydney Thunder during BBL|05?

The Thunder is a direct reflection of the cultural change the franchise has achieved both on and off the field. It's a culture of resilience, determination and freedom, with a will to go about our business the way that suits our squad. The Thunder is prepared to play a brand of cricket that challenges the status quo.

How will winning its first title change the way the Thunder is viewed by its opponents?

The other franchises will now view us as a genuine threat rather than a dangerous team to play against. I have no doubt there'll be more homework done on our squad.

What was the key to the lime greens' success?

A work in progress which began in BBL|04. Player empowerment was a big part of our success. However the leadership—both on and off the field—has been just as significant. Players, staff, families and supporters are really made to feel like they're valued stakeholders in the franchise.

Who was the Thunder's most valuable player?

Andre Russell's overs were extremely valuable. We knew he could bowl fast, we knew he was an impact player with the bat, and we knew he was athletic in the field. Usman Khawaja being available for some games was the icing on the cake for our campaign. Sadly, I don't think he'll be available for too many more BBL games due to Australian duties.

Name your magic moment from BBL|05.

Usman Khawaja's innings in the semi final. His form throughout the tournament was magical; he played a large hand in a number of games including the final. What we witnessed was a true indication of where his game is now at. As far as batting was concerned, we certainly rode on his coat-tails.

PREVIEW OF BBL|06

THE DRAW

V SYDNEY SIXERS
Spotless Stadium,
20 December 2016

V MELBOURNE RENEGADES
Etihad Stadium,
22 December 2016

V BRISBANE HEAT
Spotless Stadium,
28 December 2016

V PERTH SCORCHERS
#TheFurnace,
1 January 2017

V MELBOURNE STARS
Spotless Stadium,
4 January 2017

V HOBART HURRICANES
Blundstone Arena,
8 January 2017

V SYDNEY SIXERS
SCG, 14 January 2017

V ADELAIDE STRIKERS
Spotless Stadium,
18 January 2017

BBL|06 SQUAD

Fawad Ahmed, Aiden Blizzard, Pat Cummins, Jake Doran, Ryan Gibson, Chris Green, Usman Khawaja, Alister McDermott, Clint McKay, Kurtis Patterson, Ben Rohrer, Gurinder Sandhu, Jason Sangha, Shane Watson
Coach: Paddy Upton

THREE KEY PLAYERS

CHRIS GREEN

Born in South Africa, this tall off spinner needed to decide between a cricket career and moving to the United States after his ability on the tennis court captured the attention of a talent scout who offered him a college scholarship. Green described being around his childhood hero Jacques Kallis as a dream come true—once he overcame his 'fan-girlish' reaction to meeting the South African legend for the first time. The 23-year-old's cucumber-cool manner came to the fore in the BBL|05 Big Final, when he took 2 wickets—including Kevin Pietersen's prized scalp—and then took a great catch on the boundary before scoring an invaluable 8 runs to help steer the Thunder to the winner's dais.

PAT CUMMINS

Acknowledged as one of the bright lights of Australian cricket, Pat Cummins is determined to make up for lost time after having his last few summers crippled by injuries. The 23-year-old provided a glimpse of his potential in his only Test when—at 18—he was named man-of-the-match after spearheading Australia to victory over South Africa. Brett Lee is one of his supporters and he believes Cummins's willingness to overcome his setbacks reflects his inner strength.

KURTIS PATTERSON

At 18 years and 206 days old, Kurtis Patterson became the youngest player to score a first-class century in Australian cricket when he crunched a chanceless 157 on debut against Western Australia at the SCG in 2011. While Patterson's father Brad joked he didn't want to hear it, cricket tragics pointed out that the left-hander was tracking better than Don Bradman—a fellow product of Sydney's St George Cricket Club—at the same stage of the great man's first-class career. Bradman scored 118 on debut in 1927. While he played in one game during BBL|05, thc now 23-year-old Patterson ought to have more chances this summer.

GAME 4

SYDNEY SIXERS V HOBART HURRICANES AT THE SCG (20 DECEMBER 2015)

WHAT HAPPENED:
While Nathan Lyon, who opened the bowling for Sydney, roared, the Hurricanes whimpered. The nation's best Test spin bowler proved he's equally adept in T20 by snaring 5–23, two of which came in his first over. He dismissed Tim Paine with his fourth ball and then bamboozled Sri Lankan great Kumar Sangakkara by providing the next ball with beautiful flight. With Hobart chasing 187, the game had all but ended after Lyon's opening salvo. Former Test keeper Brad Haddin hit a whirlwind 72 from 45 balls for the Sixers, and Darren Sammy's medium-pace bowling copped terrible punishment.

WHAT THEY SAID:
'It's always a challenge in T20 because they're always trying to hit you for big sixes,' said Nathan Lyon, 'but it brings you into the game. The guys are coming at you hard.'

***Sydney Sixers** 7–186 (Haddin 72, Silk 41, Boyce 2–25) beat **Hobart Hurricanes** 91 (Bailey 62*, Lyon 5–23) by 95 runs*

GAME 5

MELBOURNE STARS V SYDNEY THUNDER AT THE MCG (20 DECEMBER 2015)

WHAT HAPPENED:
Usman Khawaja made an explosive return to the BBL in a 1-run nailbiter after injury spoilt his previous summer. His unbeaten 109 combined crude and exquisite shots, each stroke defying those experts who'd pigeonholed him as a 'traditional' player. The Thunder's 178 proved just enough to win when the Stars' James Faulkner, ranked among the game's best finishers, was on strike with 10 runs needed for victory. He hit 6 runs off the first three deliveries of Jacques Kallis's over, but fluffed an attempted ramp shot and missed the fourth. While the Stars hit another 3 runs off the last two balls, the Thunder hung on for a 1-run victory.

WHAT THEY SAID:
'[The power game] has come into my one-day game a little bit,' said Usman Khawaja. 'It's just something that hasn't been natural to me growing up.'

***Sydney Thunder** 6–178 (Khawaja 109*) beat **Melbourne Stars** 5–177 (Pietersen 76, Faulkner 45*) by 1 run*

Brad Haddin on the attack as he hammered 72 against the Hobart Hurricanes from 45 deliveries at the SCG.

Usman Khawaja kick-started his summer of runs before Christmas with an unconquered 109 against the Melbourne Stars at the MCG.

BBL|05 GAME BY GAME

GAME 6

PERTH SCORCHERS V ADELAIDE STRIKERS AT #THEFURNACE (21 DECEMBER 2015)

WHAT HAPPENED:
Defending champion Perth continued its tradition stretching back to BBL|01 of losing its season opener. This time Adelaide managed to get the better of the Scorchers in front of a 20,000-strong Perth crowd. Shaun Marsh appeared primed for a big total before he mistimed a short-pitched Michael Neser delivery and was caught on the boundary for 47. The Scorchers suffered a setback when pace bowler Nathan Coulter-Nile, who took 1–18 from three overs, left the field after injuring his shoulder while fielding. Opener Tim Ludeman set the tone for the Strikers, slamming three consecutive boundaries off paceman Joel Paris.

WHAT THEY SAID:
'We lost momentum after Shaun got out and we couldn't build a partnership through the middle and they squeezed us pretty well,' said Adam Voges.

***Adelaide Strikers** 6–152 (Jayawardene 42, Ross 38) beat **Perth Scorchers** 6–151 (Shaun Marsh 47, Voges 45*, Rashid 2–21) by 4 wickets*

GAME 7

HOBART HURRICANES V BRISBANE HEAT AT BLUNDSTONE ARENA (22 DECEMBER 2015)

WHAT HAPPENED:
Hurricanes recruit Daniel Christian tormented his former Heat teammates as they chased Hobart's 184 by backing up his tidy 2–22 with 4 catches, including a screamer in the outfield to dismiss master blaster Chris Lynn for 1. Christian was well supported by left-armer Sam Rainbird, who snared 3–37. It was a much better all-round performance for Hobart than its shocker of a season opener against the Sixers. Skipper Tim Paine helped get his team off to a flyer when he won the toss, elected to bat and struck an unconquered 87, which included four cracking sixes.

WHAT THEY SAID:
'We had a really poor first game, so it was important our senior players stood up,' said Tim Paine.

***Hobart Hurricanes** 3–184 (Paine 87*, Sangakkara 43, Bailey 40) beat **Brisbane Heat** 8–164 (Floros 42, Reardon 41, Rainbird 3–37) by 20 runs*

Getty Images

Young gun Alex Ross takes to the Perth attack during the Strikers 4-wicket victory over the Scorchers at #TheFurnace.

Safe as a bank, Dan Christian takes one of the four catches he took for the Hobart Hurricanes in their win over Brisbane.

GAME 8

MELBOURNE RENEGADES V SYDNEY SIXERS AT ETIHAD STADIUM (23 DECEMBER 2015)

WHAT HAPPENED:

After being set a daunting 173 to win on a two-paced pitch that was a minefield of inconsistent bounce, skipper Moises Henriques (62) and Michael Lumb (63) produced the highest third-wicket partnership in the Sixers' history. Their dramatic 101-run stand came after the Sixers suffered two body blows, with Brad Haddin dismissed for a golden duck and Nic Maddinson for 17. Their departures left the visitors struggling at 2–21 after only four overs. Renegades paceman Nathan Rimmington took 4–26 and triggered a late collapse when Sydney lost 4–12 in 12 balls. But Sean Abbott and Trent Lawford kept their cool to guide Sydney home.

WHAT THEY SAID:

'The boys are happy, they're buzzing, so it's pretty sweet,' said Michael Lumb. 'We'll get a lot of confidence out of that.'

***Sydney Sixers** 7–174 (Lumb 63, Henriques 62, Rimmington 4–26) beat **Melbourne Renegades** 4–172 (Gayle 46, Bravo 45*, Beaton 41*) by 3 wickets*

GAME 9

PERTH SCORCHERS V BRISBANE HEAT AT #THEFURNACE (26 DECEMBER 2015)

WHAT HAPPENED:

Cult hero Brad Hogg played a crucial role in restricting Brisbane to a paltry 7–117—and consigning them to their third straight loss—when the 44-year-old took 1–15 from his four overs. It was torture, and he was brilliantly supported by English import David Willey, who also took 1–15; Andrew Tye, who took 3–23; and Jason Behrendorff, who took 2–32. Chris Lynn was the lone light for Brisbane, scoring an unconquered 75. Michael Klinger was the backbone of Perth's win, scoring 53 not out off 42 balls as the Scorchers cruised to victory with 29 balls to spare.

WHAT THEY SAID:

'The guys are desperate to do well and we're aware of the mistakes that have happened,' said Heat coach Daniel Vettori. 'They really want the opportunity to rectify it.'

***Perth Scorchers** 1–118 (Klinger 53*, Harris 36) beat **Brisbane Heat** 7–117 (Lynn 75*, Tye 3–23) by 9 wickets*

GAME 10

SYDNEY SIXERS V MELBOURNE STARS AT THE SCG (27 DECEMBER 2015)

WHAT HAPPENED:

After seeing how Sydney's spin decimated Hobart before Christmas, the Stars used the Sixers' own tactics against them by unleashing Michael Beer, Adam Zampa and Glenn Maxwell. The trio revelled in the wicket and tied the Sixers' batters in knots, nullifying their big three—Michael Lumb (lbw to Beer for 15), Brad Haddin (dismissed by Maxwell for 2) and Nic Maddinson (bowled Zampa for 25)—from inflicting much damage. The Sixers were dismissed for 139 and an exciting Maxwell 50, allied with Peter Handscomb's 52, powered the Stars to their first win of the season.

WHAT THEY SAID:

'Without probably our best player [Kevin Pietersen] in this game, somebody had to stand up, and me and Peter filled that void,' said Glenn Maxwell.

***Melbourne Stars** 5–143 (Handscomb 52, Maxwell 50, Bollinger 2–31) beat **Sydney Sixers** 6–139 (Henriques 41, Silk 35, Hilfenhaus 2–25) by 5 wickets*

BBL|05 GAME BY GAME

GAME 11

SYDNEY THUNDER V ADELAIDE STRIKERS AT SPOTLESS STADIUM (28 DECEMBER 2015)

WHAT HAPPENED:
Sydney Thunder added weight to claims the competition's one-time easybeats had come of age when they humbled the Strikers by 7 wickets. After being set 118 to win, Aiden Blizzard and Jacques Kallis set their team on course with a 66-run opening stand. Earlier, Andre Russell rocked Adelaide by dismissing Tim Ludeman with the first ball of the innings, and the visitors never recovered. They were restricted to an agonising 47 runs in their first 10 overs. Ben Rohrer was as much cobra as fielder, displaying brilliant reflexes to run out Mahela Jayawardene and Michael Neser as Sydney won.

WHAT THEY SAID:
'Yes, it's been a brilliant start and we'll enjoy that,' said Mike Hussey, 'but there's still a long way to go, and we've got to make sure we keep our eye on the ball.'

***Sydney Thunder** 3–121 (Kallis 49*, Blizzard 35) beat **Adelaide Strikers** 9–117 (Jayawardene 21, McKay 2–18, Russell 2–28) by 7 wickets*

GAME 12

BRISBANE HEAT V HOBART HURRICANES AT THE GABBA (29 DECEMBER 2015)

WHAT HAPPENED:
One week after making a nuisance of himself against his former Brisbane team with 4 catches and 2 wickets, Hobart all-rounder Daniel Christian returned to again mastermind the Heat's downfall with a swashbuckling 56 not out from 24 deliveries that helped the Tasmania-based team reach an imposing 194. One of Christian's sixes landed 117 metres away on the grandstand roof; the shot was acknowledged by old-timers as the biggest hit they'd seen at the ground. Chris Lynn did what he could to lead Brisbane to its first win of the tournament with 101 from 51 deliveries, but he lacked support.

WHAT THEY SAID:
'I was waiting for it to come down in front of the sails and it kept going,' said Daniel Christian, 'and that's when I realised it was obviously a decent [hit].'

***Hobart Hurricanes** 4–194 (Christian 56*, Sangakkara 32) beat **Brisbane Heat** 9–179 (Lynn 101, Reed 3–31) by 15 runs*

GAME 13

MELBOURNE RENEGADES V PERTH SCORCHERS AT ETIHAD STADIUM (30 DECEMBER 2015)

WHAT HAPPENED:
Scorchers openers Shaun Marsh and Michael Klinger established a BBL record by leading Perth to the league's first-ever 10-wicket victory. They only missed breaking Luke Wright and Rob Quiney's opening stand of 172 for the Stars because they had no runs left to chase. It was Marsh's first knock since being dropped by the national selectors despite scoring 182 against the West Indies in the Hobart Test, and he definitely impressed with three sixes among his swag. It was a tough defeat for the Renegades: their openers Aaron Finch and Chris Gayle put on a thrilling 98 for the first wicket.

WHAT THEY SAID:
'You don't want to think too far ahead in this game,' said Shaun Marsh. 'I know what it can do if you do that, and I'm just going to worry about one game at a time.'

***Perth Scorchers** 0–171 (Klinger 90*, Shaun Marsh 76*) beat **Melbourne Renegades** 4–170 (Finch 72, Gayle 41, Behrendorff 2–14) by 10 wickets*

Brisbane's Chris Lynn finished the BBL|05 as King of the Sixers and let loose while scoring 101 against Hobart at the Gabba.

Opening batter Michael Klinger enjoyed plenty of highlights in BBL|05, and guiding Perth to a 10-wicket win over the Renegades was one of them.

GAME 14

ADELAIDE STRIKERS V SYDNEY SIXERS AT ADELAIDE OVAL (31 DECEMBER 2015)

WHAT HAPPENED:

Travis Head dragged the Strikers off the canvas and belted them to an improbable victory. The match had everything, including a verbal donnybrook between the Sixers' Brad Haddin and fast bowler Ben Laughlin, who was adamant that Haddin should have walked when caught behind. It was Head, however, who ignited the real fireworks. When Sean Abbott shaped to bowl the 18th over, the Strikers needed 51 runs to win and Head dramatically reduced that, crunching 27 rapid-fire runs off the fast bowler. Adelaide required 13 and the 22-year-old hit each of the first three deliveries of Abbott's final over for six to record a stunning win.

WHAT THEY SAID:

'For me this season has been about trying to go out to prove to a few people that the belief they've given me is right.' said Travis Head.

***Adelaide Strikers** 5–182 (Head 101*, Dwarshuis 3–25) beat **Sydney Sixers** 5–176 (Haddin 54*, Cowan 43, Rashid 3–34) by 5 wickets*

GAME 15

HOBART HURRICANES V SYDNEY THUNDER AT BLUNDSTONE ARENA (1 JANUARY 2016)

WHAT HAPPENED:

A record crowd witnessed a phenomenal display of pace bowling by former Test spearhead Shaun Tait. He blasted out two of the world's best T20 batsmen, Jacques Kallis and Shane Watson, in the first over. With Sydney reeling at 2–1, Mike Hussey's 71 was inspiring, but ultimately counted for little as his team unravelled under the pressure. Hobart took a team hat-trick after Hussey fell, Chris Hartley was run out by Daniel Christian and Tim Paine took a classic catch to dismiss Chris Green. The Thunder lost 5–13—including 4–6 off seven balls—to fall 11 runs short of victory.

WHAT THEY SAID:

'I think even when we got [Hussey] out the game was on the line,' said George Bailey. 'A couple of clutch overs from Jakey Reed and Shaun Tait, really set the tone for us.'

***Hobart Hurricanes** 6–163 (Bailey 56*, Wells 27, McKay 4–28) beat **Sydney Thunder** 9–152 (Hussey 71, Tait 3–16, Reed 3–35) by 11 runs*

BBL|05 GAME BY GAME

GAME 16

MELBOURNE STARS V MELBOURNE RENEGADES AT THE MCG (2 JANUARY 2016)

WHAT HAPPENED:
Luke Wright slammed an unbeaten 109 off 63 deliveries, but the most talked about statistic from Melbourne's derby was the 80,883-strong crowd, which annihilated the 52,637 record set in Adelaide during BBL|04. Those who attended witnessed some tremendous cricket, although the match-up between monster hitters Chris Gayle and Kevin Pietersen was a fizzer. Renegades veteran Cameron White scored 54 against his old team while John Hastings took an impressive 4–29 for the Stars. It was Wright who stole centre stage, however, with a barnstorming effort worthy of a huge crowd.

WHAT THEY SAID:
'We had a feeling it was going to be big tonight, but obviously not that big—and [in] a derby,' said Luke Wright. 'It's probably one of the best cricketing moments I've had in my life.'

Melbourne Stars *3–163 (Wright 109*) beat* ***Melbourne Renegades*** *7–161 (White 54, Hastings 4–29) by 7 wickets*

GAME 17

PERTH SCORCHERS V SYDNEY SIXERS AT #THEFURNACE (2 JANUARY 2016)

WHAT HAPPENED:
Perth thumped the Sixers in a one-sided replay of BBL|04's nailbiting final. Perth's renowned bowling attack lived up to its reputation as the best in the league, restricting the Sixers to 112. Spearheaded by David Willey's 3–22, the pack didn't allow the Sixers to relax; Andrew Tye (2–21), Jason Behrendorff (2–24) and Joel Paris (1–23) enjoyed turning the screws. Shaun Marsh scored an unbeaten 63 as he made short work of the win. When Michael Klinger fell to Sean Abbott for 28 it was the first time in two matches the Scorchers had lost a wicket.

WHAT THEY SAID:
'Credit to the lads,' said David Willey. 'We're bowling together as a unit, and that makes it very difficult for the opposition when all four of us seamers and obviously Hoggy as well are putting it in the right areas.'

Perth Scorchers *1–114 (Shaun Marsh 63*) beat* ***Sydney Sixers*** *8–112 (Lumb 47, Willey 3–22) by 9 wickets*

GAME 18

BRISBANE HEAT V SYDNEY THUNDER AT THE GABBA (3 JANUARY 2016)

WHAT HAPPENED:
Chris Lynn hammered a 32-ball 75 in driving rain to allow the Heat to steam past the Thunder's 186. In doing so he guided Brisbane to their first win of the season. Adding insult to the Thunder's injury, after the umpires insisted play could continue in what some thought were dangerous conditions, they fumbled the chances Lynn offered when he was on 57 and 66. Lynn also used this match to become only the fourth batter to pass the 1000-run BBL barrier, 24 of them coming off a Gurinder Sandhu over. Michael Hussey starred again for the Thunder, hitting 56.

WHAT THEY SAID:
'That's a nice innings before a one-day team is named,' said former Test captain Ricky Ponting of Lynn's performance.

Brisbane Heat *4–189 (Lynn 75, Peirson 40) beat* ***Sydney Thunder*** *5–186 (Hussey 56, Watson 46) by 6 wickets*

GAME 19

HOBART HURRICANES V MELBOURNE RENEGADES AT BLUNDSTONE ARENA (4 JANUARY 2016)

WHAT HAPPENED:

With some brutal batting, the Renegades destroyed the Hurricanes as they rampaged to a 5-wicket victory with 36 deliveries in hand. Aaron Finch's 60 and Chris Gayle's 41 from 15 balls elevated them on the points table to just one win from fourth place. It was a disastrous blow for Hobart, who would have seized top spot had they won. Daniel Christian excelled, but apart from Ben Dunk's whirlwind innings he received no support. Chris Gayle's 'Don't blush, baby' pick-up line to reporter Mel McLaughlin during a live TV interview was widely condemned. He was fined $10,000 and many thought it was unlikely he'd return for BBL|06.

WHAT THEY SAID:

'Today we weren't prepared to take risks,' said Tim Paine. 'It was a really poor approach to our batting. We had no intent at the start.'

***Melbourne Renegades** 5–144 (Finch 60, Gayle 41, Boyce 3–34) beat **Hobart Hurricanes** 5–140 (Christian 58, Dunk 37) by 5 wickets*

GAME 20

ADELAIDE STRIKERS V PERTH SCORCHERS AT ADELAIDE OVAL (5 JANUARY 2016)

WHAT HAPPENED:

When Sri Lanka's Mahela Jayawardene replaced power hitter Craig Simmons, he produced an aggressive innings that allowed the Strikers to surge to the top of the competition ladder. He hammered 57 from 37 deliveries, opening his shoulder blades to hit two sixes and seven fours. Travis Head continued with his New Year's Eve heroics, nailing an unbeaten 51. Perth's Joel Paris provided a highlight in the field when he secured a catch while flat on his back after appearing to have fluffed it. A purple patch from openers Shaun Marsh (4) and Michael Klinger (15) was disrupted by their cheap dismissals.

WHAT THEY SAID:

'When you're opening the batting, you've got a bit more freedom,' said Mahela Jayawardene. 'The way the wicket was playing, it was quite easy for me to change gears.'

***Adelaide Strikers** 2–174 (Jayawardene 57, Head 51*) beat **Perth Scorchers** 138 (Rashid 3–23) by 36 runs*

The Melbourne Stars Luke Wright proving why he's 'Mr Wright' with a cracking 109 runs in front of 80,883 spectators at the MCG.

Aaron Finch spearheaded the Renegades to a dominant 5-wicket win with 36 balls in hand against the Hurricanes in Hobart.

BBL|05 GAME BY GAME

GAME 21

MELBOURNE STARS V HOBART HURRICANES AT THE MCG (6 JANUARY 2016)

WHAT HAPPENED:
Stars opener Luke Wright followed up on his century with yet another match-winning knock. Wright's performances emphasised why the Englishman is one of the world's most sought-after T20 players, with his record showing he also plays in New Zealand, India, Bangladesh and Dubai. Wright's 99-run stand with Glenn Maxwell ensured the Stars recovered from a shaky start to their 125-run chase. Hurricanes veteran George Bailey, another friend of Hobden's, blasted 55 in a brave stand that came on top of his selection in Australia's one-day team. Stars leg spinner Adam Zampa continued with his outstanding form, taking 2–18.

WHAT THEY SAID:
'I feel like from the back of the Shield season that I've been scoring some runs and been reasonably consistent in the BBL,' said George Bailey.

***Melbourne Stars** 2–126 (Maxwell 56*, Wright 51*) beat **Hobart Hurricanes** 124 (Bailey 55, Zampa 2–18, Boland 2–26) by 8 wickets*

GAME 22

SYDNEY THUNDER V PERTH SCORCHERS AT SPOTLESS STADIUM (7 JANUARY 2016)

WHAT HAPPENED:
Just as Sydney Thunders' long-suffering supporters dared to believe they had a team that could be title contenders, Perth's young guns spoiled the party. Ashton Agar (68) and Cameron Bancroft (72) followed coach Justin Langer's demand for his middle order to perform by smashing their maiden BBL half-centuries. Their efforts were brilliantly supported by Andrew Tye and Jason Behrendorff, who each took 3 wickets as the Thunder staggered to 145. All-rounder Andre Russell was the pick of the home team, with five massive sixes among his cavalier 42 runs, while his 2–31 made him the league's leading wicket-taker.

WHAT THEY SAID:
'That is my first score in the tournament,' said Ashton Agar. 'I've been hitting the ball pretty well in the nets and hopefully I can go on with it from here.'

***Perth Scorchers** 5–175 (Bancroft 72, Agar 68, Russell 2–31) beat **Sydney Thunder** 9–145 (Russell 42, Tye 3–22, Behrendorff 3–26) by 30 runs*

While he battled a back problem Jason Behrendorff performed well, taking 3–26 against the Thunder at Spotless Stadium.

Mahela Jayawardene defied the discomfort of a strained quadriceps to score a half-century and guide Adelaide home against Brisbane.

GAME 23

BRISBANE HEAT V ADELAIDE STRIKERS AT THE GABBA (8 JANUARY 2016)

WHAT HAPPENED:
Mahela Jayawardene overcame a quadriceps strain to strike a man-of-the-match 53 and help Adelaide wrestle back the competition lead. His opening partner Tim Ludeman scored 57, but Travis Head and Brisbane's big hitter Chris Lynn (who scored 34) were the main talking points amid a push for their selection in Australia's World T20 squad. Head helped quash Brisbane's faint finals hopes with a blistering 50, ensuring the Strikers won with eight balls and as many wickets in hand. It was the first time Head was dismissed in three innings, ending a rare streak that included 202 runs and a miracle century.

WHAT THEY SAID:
'You can't bat as well as they are and not have your name up in lights,' said national selector Mark Waugh of Head and Lynn.

***Adelaide Strikers** 2–179 (Ludeman 57*, Jayawardene 53, Head 50) beat **Brisbane Heat** 6–175 (Peirson 51, Reardon 40, Rashid 2–17) by 8 wickets*

GAME 24

MELBOURNE RENEGADES V MELBOURNE STARS AT ETIHAD STADIUM (9 JANUARY 2016)

WHAT HAPPENED:
The Stars' chase was delayed as officials waited for the smoke from the fireworks to disperse, but when Marcus Stoinis and Luke Wright shaped up they were focused, plundering 32 runs from the opening three overs. Two deliveries in the 14th over typified the Renegades' night, when Kevin Pietersen, who scored a match-winning 67, survived a confident appeal from Dwayne Bravo and then, after a horrible mix-up, the ball he skied to deep cover fell safely. 'Gades batsman Chris Gayle—still in hot water for his McLaughlin interview—became one of Stoinis's three victims when dismissed for a meek 21.

WHAT THEY SAID:
'We've got the momentum now—we've won four in a row,' said Adam Zampa. 'It's a bit of a theme with the Stars; we start off quite slow but we've got a bit of momentum.'

***Melbourne Stars** 2–156 (Pietersen 67*, Handscomb 39*) beat **Melbourne Renegades** 6–155 (Bravo 59*, Stoinis 3–11) by 8 wickets*

GAME 25

HOBART HURRICANES V PERTH SCORCHERS AT BLUNDSTONE ARENA (10 JANUARY 2016)

WHAT HAPPENED:
Hobart's Darren Sammy, who injured his hamstring when he took two quick runs, needed to belt 16 runs off Perth paceman Andrew Tye's final over. He limped through for another double off the next ball, and while the third ball was a Tye special—a searing yorker—Sammy smacked a wide delivery for six. With six needed from the final two deliveries he swung . . . missed . . . and Jonathan Wells was run out. The last delivery was thrashed for four but it wasn't enough. Perth's Michael Carberry, finally given a game, engineered the win with 62 runs before being dismissed by a 150 km/h Shaun Tait missile.

WHAT THEY SAID:
'I just had to sit and wait my turn, but it gave me some time to go away and work in the nets,' said Michael Carberry. 'The last week I've been feeling in good touch.'

***Perth Scorchers** 5–173 (Carberry 62, Klinger 36) beat **Hobart Hurricanes** 6–172 (Paine 57, Agar 2–38) by 1 run*

BBL|05 GAME BY GAME

GAME 26

SYDNEY SIXERS V BRISBANE HEAT AT THE SCG (10 JANUARY 2016)

WHAT HAPPENED:
Brisbane won their second match of the season by 6 runs, officially ending the Sixers' injury-riddled campaign. Sydney's pace bowler Sean Abbott, however, recovered from his New Year's Eve nightmare in Adelaide, bagging 3–8. While Brisbane's Joe Burns slammed an impressive 60—in his second BBL match of the season—and Lendl Simmons struck 54, Abbott's 12 deliveries were extraordinary. Michael Lumb and Brad Haddin's efforts to keep the Sixers' season alive were 'kindly' assisted by the Heat, which dropped 5 catches. The Queenslander debutant leg spinner Mitchell Swepson captured 2–26.

WHAT THEY SAID:
'It was as pleasing an over . . . if not two overs . . . I've seen all season, if not a couple of years,' said Sixers bowling coach Geoff Lawson of Abbott's performance.

***Brisbane Heat** 8–162 (Burns 60, Simmons 54, Abbott 3–8) beat **Sydney Sixers** 8–156 (Lumb 47, Haddin 42, Swepson 2–26) by 6 runs*

GAME 27

SYDNEY THUNDER V MELBOURNE RENEGADES AT SPOTLESS STADIUM (11 JANUARY 2016)

WHAT HAPPENED:
After a week of criticism for his 'Don't blush' interview, Chris Gayle was in trouble again when he refused to run after hitting a Clint McKay delivery 90 metres to long on. Commentator Ricky Ponting described it as the most 'ridiculous' cricket he'd seen. The controversy dominated a tremendous Renegades victory, set up by Cameron White with his fighting 61. An extraordinary dismissal occurred earlier in the match: Andre Russell swung around his bat and hit his stumps when a Nathan Rimmington bumper hit him on the shoulder and ricocheted onto his helmet.

WHAT THEY SAID:
'We just want him to entertain,' said Cameron White of Gayle. 'I'd really like to see him play like he did against the Hurricanes [when he scored 41 off 15 balls]—I want to see that Chris Gayle.'

***Melbourne Renegades** 5–176 (White 61, Bravo 47) beat **Sydney Thunder** 5–173 (Khawaja 62, Watson 62, Bravo 2–26) by 5 wickets*

GAME 28

ADELAIDE STRIKERS V HOBART HURRICANES AT ADELAIDE OVAL (13 JANUARY 2016)

WHAT HAPPENED:
Jake Lehmann, the son of Australian coach Darren Lehmann, needed to hit a four off his first-ever BBL ball faced, but the 23-year-old Strikers left-hander lifted Simon Milenko over long off for six to send Adelaide to the top of the ladder and seal a home semi final. It was a cruel blow for Milenko, who was Hobart's best with 3–25. The Hurricanes, who won the toss and elected to bat, wilted under pressure. Strikers opener Tim Ludeman scored an unconquered 57, while Brad Hodge's promising start was ended by Shaun Tait, who reached 155 km/h during a fiery spell.

WHAT THEY SAID:
'I had 100 per cent faith in [Lehmann] when he went out,' said Greg West. 'He wasn't nervous, he was good to go.'

***Adelaide Strikers** 4–146 (Ludeman 57*, Milenko 3–25) beat **Hobart Hurricanes** 143 (Paine 45, Neser 3–26) by 6 wickets*

Nathan Rimmington bends his back in the Melbourne Renegades 5-wicket win over the BBL's eventual champions, the Sydney Thunder.

Brisbane's Samuel Badree can't contain his delight after dismissing Kevin Pietersen in the Heat's 56-run victory over the Melbourne Stars.

GAME 29

MELBOURNE STARS V BRISBANE HEAT AT THE MCG (14 JANUARY 2016)

WHAT HAPPENED:
Chris Lynn went ballistic, hitting five consecutive sixes off Ben Hilfenhaus, while brilliant leg spinner Samuel Badree backed up Lynn's performance, taking 5–22. The Heat was sent in to bat on a wet 'n' wild Melbourne night, and while Jimmy Peirson fell for nought, Lynn combined with Lendl Simmons to score 78 in the powerplay. After hammering Daniel Worrall out of the attack, Lynn then savaged Hilfenhaus, hitting one ball for a soaring 123-metre six over deep square leg and into the stands. Despite the magnitude of the victory, Brisbane had no hope of qualifying for the finals.

WHAT THEY SAID:
'I've played confident, fear-free cricket throughout this campaign,' said Chris Lynn, 'and I just wanted to do the same again tonight.'

***Brisbane Heat** 7–188 (Lynn 56, Simmons 44) beat **Melbourne Stars** 9–132 (Gulbis 61*, Badree 5–22) by 56 runs*

GAME 30

SYDNEY SIXERS V SYDNEY THUNDER AT THE SCG (16 JANUARY 2016)

WHAT HAPPENED:
Mike Hussey left the SCG for the final time a winner after the Thunder dominated the Sixers. While the 46-run victory gave the Thunder every opportunity to qualify for the finals, they endured an agonising wait for other matches to go their way. Nevertheless, the win over the Sixers was special. Batting first, Hussey's men scored 202 on the back of a scintillating Shane Watson 66, a whirlwind Andre Russell 46 and clever 41 by Hussey. Clint McKay, Chris Green and Fawad Ahmed all took 3 wickets for the Thunder, but Nic Maddinson's 70 demonstrated why the Sixers' stand-in skipper started the tournament the No. 1–ranked batsman.

WHAT THEY SAID:
'We turned up tonight without two of our best players,' said Mike Hussey, 'and we put on a great show and a great performance.'

***Sydney Thunder** 5–202 (Watson 66, Russell 46, Hussey 41, Abbott 2–41) beat **Sydney Sixers** 156 (Maddinson 70, McKay 3–16, Green 3–27, Fawad 3–39) by 46 runs*

BBL|05 GAME BY GAME

GAME 31

PERTH SCORCHERS V MELBOURNE STARS AT #THEFURNACE (16 JANUARY 2016)

WHAT HAPPENED:
The Stars needed to defeat the defending champions Perth—at home—by 38 runs to secure a home semi final, and superb performances by Daniel Worrall (3–15), Ben Hilfenhaus (3–17) and Adam Zampa (2–16) ensured they won by 52. It appeared mission impossible when the Stars were restricted to 9–146, but aside from Adam Voges' 46, Perth capitulated. The Stars also enjoyed some luck: Perth's Michael Carberry was dismissed when the ball deflected from his glove onto his wicket, while Cameron Bancroft fell when the ball rebounded off the keeper's gloves onto the stumps.

WHAT THEY SAID:
'I got the message about 25 times that we needed to keep them around 108 for a home semi,' said David Hussey, 'and we were lucky enough to get some late wickets there.'

Melbourne Stars *9–146 (Hussey 36, Dixon 3–32) beat* ***Perth Scorchers*** *94 (Voges 46*, Worrall 3–15, Hilfenhaus 3–17) by 52 runs*

GAME 32

MELBOURNE RENEGADES V ADELAIDE STRIKERS AT ETIHAD STADIUM (18 JANUARY 2016)

WHAT HAPPENED:
Adelaide qualified for the semi, but Chris Gayle commanded the attention when he took only 12 balls to hit the BBL's fastest-ever 50. It couldn't help the Renegades reach the semi final, however; apart from falling 27 runs short, in order to qualify they needed to reach the Strikers' 5–170 within 16 overs. Gayle's effort was a thrill a ball, as he hit seven sixes, four of them from consecutive deliveries in the opening over. After three overs the Renegades were 1–53, but their explosive start couldn't be sustained. Travis Head's part-time spin signalled the end when he dismissed Cameron White and Dwayne Bravo in the fourth over.

WHAT THEY SAID:
'We all know Chris Gayle is an amazing striker of the ball. When he's on, he's on,' said Jason Gillespie.'

Adelaide Strikers *5–170 (Ludeman 49, Dean 48, Doherty 2–30) beat* ***Melbourne Renegades*** *143 (Gayle 56, Head 3–16) by 27 runs*

FIRST SEMI FINAL

ADELAIDE STRIKERS V SYDNEY THUNDER AT ADELAIDE OVAL (21 JANUARY 2016)

WHAT HAPPENED:
Usman Khawaja, a foundation Thunder player, stole the show as he guided his team to a breakthrough Big Final berth with a pristine unbeaten 104. He treated the Thunder's biggest moment like a schoolboy might a lunchtime hit-out, smashing 13 boundaries and three sixes to run down the 160 required. His assault was so brutal, the Adelaide crowd wildly applauded a rare Michael Neser dot ball. Earlier, the Thunder shocked the BBL's stand-out team with early breakthroughs, most significantly Adelaide's danger man Travis Head being dismissed by Clint McKay for 23. Alex Ross scored a brave 47 before falling to McKay.

WHAT THEY SAID:
'[Khawaja] is so relaxed and so clear in his mind about how he's going about it at the moment,' said Mike Hussey.

Sydney Thunder *2–160 (Khawaja 104*) beat* ***Adelaide Strikers*** *7–159 (Ross 47, McKay 3–44) by 8 wickets*

SECOND SEMI FINAL

MELBOURNE STARS V PERTH SCORCHERS AT THE MCG (22 JANUARY 2016)

WHAT HAPPENED:

The Melbourne Stars finally qualified for their first BBL Big Final (their four previous semi finals having ended in heartache) with a comprehensive win over Perth. Daniel Worrall used his swing to star during the powerplay and at the death, while Adam Zampa's nagging leg spin and Michael Beer's spin caused headaches. Perth's Adam Voges (52) and ever-reliable Michael Klinger (44) provided their bowlers with something to defend. But Kevin Pietersen steered Melbourne to victory with a measured innings that ensured the scoreboard ticked over when boundaries were scarce.

WHAT THEY SAID:

'We all know—the guys who are the fringe players—that we have to come in and provide something,' said Daniel Worrall.

***Melbourne Stars** 3–140 (Pietersen 62, Stoinis 44) beat **Perth Scorchers** 7–139 (Voges 52, Klinger 44, Worrall 3–25) by 7 wickets*

BIG FINAL

MELBOURNE STARS V SYDNEY THUNDER AT THE MCG (24 JANUARY 2016)

WHAT HAPPENED:

He couldn't make Australia's one-day team, despite a stunning T20 campaign, but yet another Usman Khawaja run spree helped the Sydney Thunder complete the BBL's greatest fairytale of all, when the team once dismissed as the competition's problem child won the title. While Khawaja scored 70 from 40 balls, he received plenty of help early in the innings from Jacques Kallis, as the two used the powerplay to whittle away 62 of the 177 runs needed for victory. Their powerful stand ended on 86, and while there was a run of wickets—including Hussey for 18—Ben Rohrer secured an emotion-charged victory with a big six.

WHAT THEY SAID:

'This is what you play for,' said Mike Hussey. 'This is what you hope to achieve, but when you actually do it . . . it takes a bit of time to sink in.'

***Sydney Thunder** 7–181 (Khawaja 70, Stoinis 3–30) beat **Melbourne Stars** 9–176 (Pietersen 74, Watson 2–17, Green 2–37) by 3 wickets*

Kevin Pietersen scored a masterful 62 in tough conditions to navigate the Melbourne Stars to their 7-wicket semi-final victory over Perth.

Ben Rohrer can't contain his excitement after striking a big six that sealed the title for his Sydney Thunder over the Melbourne Stars.

THE WBBL REVOLUTION

THE SUMMER WHEN WOMEN'S CRICKET EXPLODED WITH ANTICIPATION AND COLOUR

'WE TRIED TO FORM THE BEST [T20] COMPETITION AND I THINK WE ACHIEVED THAT'

Cricket Australia official, and women's cricket legend, Belinda Clark.

After a season in which her sport FINALLY received widespread publicity, enjoyed bumper television ratings and record crowds—which included 500 people lining up for a game before the gates opened—superstar Meg Lanning declared there's no turning back for women's cricket after the runaway success of Rebel WBBL|01.

Lanning, acknowledged by the likes of former Australian captain Michael Clarke as a 'genuine' talent, was named the best player of the inaugural tournament. However, the rapid rise of women's cricket through the WBBL was a far greater source of excitement for her.

'It is going to make a massive difference,' Lanning said of the competition. 'Whenever the games were screened on Network Ten the ratings showed there were great audiences while decent-sized crowds turned out to watch. And that's what we're after! We want to take cricket to more people. We haven't had that opportunity before and the ratings proved that there really is a market for women's sport.'

WBBL|01 started with an explosion of colour and anticipation when the Brisbane Heat and Melbourne Stars played two games against each other in one day at Melbourne's Junction Oval.

Lanning justified her ranking as the world's No. 1 batter with a rapid-fire 90 off 58 balls in the opening match and a masterful 75 in the afternoon game. However, the 24-year-old recalled there was more at stake that day than statistics and points.

Meg Lanning enhanced her status as the world's No. 1 female cricketer with her haul of 560 runs for the Melbourne Stars. The Heat's Beth Mooney watches on as Lanning cracks a delivery for six at Junction Oval.

'It was really pleasing to have lots of young boys and girls at that first game. It meant a lot to have them cheering us on,' she said. 'As cricketers we saw it as an opportunity to give them something to aspire to.'

The public embraced the competition and apart from attracting over 70,000 fans to WBBL matches staged around the country, the television ratings painted the following promising picture:

- An average audience of 231,000 watched the 10 televised matches.
- A total audience of 2.56 million watched the games screened by Network Ten.
- The audience for the Sydney derby peaked at 496,000, making the WBBL the No. 1 program across all channel's for its time slot.

Talk of forming the WBBL started in 2014 when the Southern Stars won their third successive World T20 title, but it wasn't until February 2015 that Cricket Australia acknowledged there needed to be greater opportunities for their female players to showcase their skills.

Nevertheless, there was plenty to plough through in the 10 months from the announcement to Brisbane Heat's Courtney Hill running in to bowl the first ball of the 59-match competition that was ultimately won by the Sydney Thunder in a nail-biter.

As each BBL team prepared to field a women's side, separate Twitter accounts for the WBBL and its teams were established; the states released their players to become free agents; Network Ten agreed to televise some matches; and franchises were allowed to field five Southern Stars and three overseas recruits.

While some people described the move as a gamble, sporting retailer Rebel provided the WBBL with corporate clout—and confidence—by signing on to sponsor the tournament.

It proved to be a masterstroke as the world's best female players—including England's Charlotte Edwards, Sarah Taylor and Jamaican excitement machine Stafanie Taylor—descended upon Australia for a summer many believe has changed the face of the sport forever.

Adelaide Strikers

FOUNDED:	2015
COLOUR:	Blue
HOME GROUNDS:	Adelaide Oval and Adelaide Oval No. 2
GAME RESULTS WBBL|01:	**Wins:** 6 • **Losses:** 8
POSITION FINISHED WBBL|01:	Seventh
MOST WBBL|01 RUNS:	Sarah Taylor 393 **HS:** 78* • **Av:** 32.75 • **S/R:** 115.24
MOST WBBL|01 WICKETS:	Sarah Coyte 14 **BBI:** 3–12 • **Av:** 18.28 • **Econ:** 5.90 • **S/R:** 18.5
MOST WBBL|01 CATCHES:	Sarah Taylor 6
WBBL|01 SQUAD:	Lauren Ebsary (c), Samantha Betts, Sarah Coyte, Sophie Devine, Stacy-Ann King, Tahlia McGrath, Tegan McPharlin, Shelley Nitschke, Bridget Patterson, Hannah Perry, Alex Price, Megan Schutt, Sarah Taylor, Miranda Veringmeier, Amanda-Jade Wellington **Coach:** Andrea McCauley
PLAYER OF THE YEAR:	Sarah Taylor

Early fireworks: The Adelaide Strikers, seen by many as the team to beat in WBBL|01, celebrate their New Year's Eve victory over the Perth Scorchers at Adelaide Oval.

SEASON SNAPSHOT WBBL|01

Adelaide started WBBL|01 identified by some experts as the team to beat because of the strength of its batting line-up. It was headlined by England's run-scoring machine Sarah Taylor, and members of the triumphant South Australian Women's National Cricket League (WNCL) squad that ended New South Wales's decade-long stranglehold on the trophy. The Andrea McCauley–coached Strikers paid a hefty price, however, for losing their opening four matches because, try as they might, they couldn't make up the lost ground in a roller-coaster of a season. Some blamed the team's two-run loss to the Hurricanes in their opening match as the reason they just missed out on the finals. Nevertheless, there were some bright spots: Taylor was outstanding, amassing 393 runs; Sarah Coyte performed brilliantly batting at No. 3 later in the tournament; while New Zealander Sophie Devine's unbeaten 47 off 15 deliveries against the Stars was a show stopper.

PLAYER'S VERDICT

The Strikers finished seventh but they were only one victory away from the finals. All-rounder Shelley Nitschke recalls the high cost of a slow start.

What did the Adelaide Strikers gain from WBBL|01?

We missed the jump last year, the season got away from us early in the piece and we couldn't pull it back. We learnt a lot, especially about consistency, and we'll hit the ground running in WBBL|02.

How do you develop that consistency?

T20 is all about consistency. We just need to look at having some more contributors. Adelaide had some very good individual performances but we needed a bit more from some players—myself included. If we can get those extra contributions it means our team's consistency will fall into place.

What did other teams learn from the Sydney Thunder and Sixers title decider?

The difference between the Thunder and us was they were solid throughout the whole season. They had players who had great summers but everyone was chipping in and got the job done. What we saw in the [closely fought] final was no matter how your season goes you're half a chance to win it.

Describe the pressure of a WBBL match.

I found everything was magnified in the WBBL. If you miss a beat with a field placement or a bowling change it can have a much bigger impact than it might in a 50-over game. All of your decisions, any little error, can have such a big impact. It's constant, intense pressure.

Who was Adelaide's best player?

I'd say Sarah Taylor, but she was closely followed by Sarah Coyte. [Taylor] was outstanding with the bat and some of her stumpings were amazing. Coytie was as good with the bat and ball but in a toss-up I'd just give the nod to Taylor.

Can you name your WBBL|01 magic moment?

I'll never forget Sophie Devine's effort to hit 47 off 15 balls when we played the Stars at Junction Oval in Melbourne. That was my special moment.

PREVIEW OF WBBL|02

THE DRAW

V MELBOURNE RENEGADES
Sydney,
10 & 11 December 2016

V SYDNEY THUNDER
Penrith, 16 & 17 December 2016

V HOBART HURRICANES
Adelaide,
26 & 27 December 2016

V PERTH SCORCHERS
Adelaide Oval,
31 December 2016

V SYDNEY SIXERS
Adelaide, 2 & 3 January 2017

V MELBOURNE STARS
Melbourne, 10 January 2017

V MELBOURNE STARS
Perth, 13 January 2017

V PERTH SCORCHERS
#TheFurnace,
14 January 2017

V BRISBANE HEAT
The Gabba,
20 & 21 January 2017

WBBL|02 SQUAD

Samantha Betts, Sarah Coyte, Sophie Devine, Tahlia McGrath, Tegan McPharlin, Shelley Nitschke, Bridget Patterson, Katelyn Pope, Alex Price, Megan Schutt, Amanda-Jade Wellington **Coach:** Andrea McCauley

THREE KEY PLAYERS

SARAH COYTE

Sarah Coyte's initiation to cricket was a tough one, having to face up to the pace bowling of her older brother Scott and twin Adam—both of whom would eventually represent New South Wales and the Sydney Thunder. She wasn't spared the tough stuff, copping plenty of bruises in their backyard Tests. Coyte, a valued member of the Southern Stars and Strikers, has no complaints, though. She says her brothers played an important role in preparing her for international cricket and the pressures of the WBBL, where she took 14 wickets for Adelaide last summer.

MEGAN SCHUTT

Megan Schutt joined forces with her idol Ellyse Perry to spearhead Australia's sixth World Cup triumph in 2013, taking 2–38 in the final against the West Indies at Mumbai. The effort, which came only a few months after she made her debut for the Southern Stars against New Zealand, emphasised she was a star on the rise. She took 15 wickets for the tournament, and some of women's cricket's biggest names were among her haul. In 2015 the fast bowler from Sturt helped Australia win the Ashes on English soil for the first time since 2001. She took 10 wickets in WBBL|01, including 3–8 against Hobart.

SOPHIE DEVINE

While Sophie Devine has represented New Zealand in cricket and hockey, her childhood dream was to become a member of the famous All Black rugby team after playing 'heaps' of games with her brother on the front lawn of the family home. Devine played most of her junior cricket in boys' teams, but on one of the rare occasions she played in a girls representative XI officials attempted to ban her by citing her pace bowling as a 'health and safety' concern. Devine is a role model for people battling diabetes because she's proof people suffering from the disease can enjoy an active lifestyle.

WHAT'S IN STORE FOR THIS SEASON

BEST-CASE SCENARIO

That Adelaide Strikers, who boast numerous players from South Australia's Women's National Cricket League team, replicate the Scorpion's 2015 success and win the WBBL|02 crown. Adelaide's roster suggests they are a semi finals-calibre team, but their batters must provide greater support to the likes of Sophie Devine, who last summer enhanced her reputation as a match winner by doing such things as smashing 47 off 15 deliveries against the Stars.

BIGGEST CHALLENGE

To regain the 'team to beat' tag they started WBBL|01 with via some big performances. The Strikers boast a core of strong batters, with Devine finishing last summer as the tournament's Queen of Sixers after clearing the boundary on 10 occasions. England international Sarah Taylor scored an impressive 393 runs, but Adelaide's top five must step up.

Getty Images

Sophie Devine, who dreamt of being an All Black when she was a little girl, was brutal for the Adelaide Strikers during WBBL|01. Her total of 224 runs including an unconquered 47 off 15 balls.

ADELAIDE Strikers

ADELAIDE OVAL

ESTABLISHED
1873

CAPACITY
53,583

PLAYING AREA
183 × 134 m

FIRST BBL MATCH
ADELAIDE STRIKERS V MELBOURNE RENEGADES
(18 December 2011)

FIRST TEST
AUSTRALIA V ENGLAND
(1884)

Adelaide Oval was established as the South Australian Cricket Association's (SACA's) headquarters in 1871, but the inaugural first-class match wasn't played there until 1877, between South Australia and Tasmania. Considered one of the world's most picturesque cricket grounds, its $575 million 2008–14 redevelopment was hailed as an architectural triumph, catering for the demands of the modern world without affecting its unique historical charm. The oval's original dimensions were 190 by 125 metres, curiously long and narrow for a cricket field, and it favoured batsmen who played square of the wicket. Until the SACA made the boundaries shorter, it wasn't uncommon for batsmen to run 4 or even 5. Adelaide Oval has a reputation as a batter's paradise.

Getty Images

FOUNDED:	2015
COLOUR:	Teal
HOME GROUNDS:	The Gabba and Allan Border Field
GAME RESULTS WBBL|01:	**Wins:** 7 • **Losses:** 7
POSITION FINISHED WBBL|01:	Sixth
MOST WBBL|01 RUNS:	Beth Mooney 400 **HS:** 64 • **Av:** 33.33 • **S/R:** 103.62
MOST WBBL|01 WICKETS:	Delissa Kimmince 17 **BBI:** 3–19 • **Av:** 14.64 • **Econ:** 7.58 • **S/R:** 11.5
MOST WBBL|01 CATCHES:	Beth Mooney 11
WBBL|01 SQUAD:	Delissa Kimmince (c), Jemma Barsby, Ashleigh Barty, Kate Cross, Holly Ferling, Jodie Fields, Abi Godfrey, Grace Harris, Laura Harris, Courtney Hill, Sammy-Jo Johnson, Jess Jonassen, Beth Mooney, Norma Ovasuru, Kirby Short, Lauren Winfield **Coach:** Andy Richards
PLAYER OF THE YEAR:	Beth Mooney

Feeling the Heat: Brisbane needed more consistency in WBBL|01 but they still enjoyed a number of highlights throughout the tournament.

SEASON SNAPSHOT WBBL|01

Brisbane's Grace Harris scored the WBBL's first century and Beth Mooney accumulated 400 runs to finish among the tournament's top run-scorers. However, the Heat's failure to consistently share the runs among the batters hurt them as they finished in sixth place. On the contrary, there weren't any problems sharing wickets with five Brisbane bowlers—spearheaded by Delissa Kimmince with 17—finishing the tournament with over 10 wickets. The only other team to achieve that was the Sydney Thunder, the eventual champions. There were some great highlights, including a thrilling 14-run victory over the Thunder and two victories over competition runners-up the Sixers. While Brisbane's inaugural squad was rich in talent, former junior Wimbledon tennis champion Ashleigh Barty was the focus of immense media attention after switching sports. The then 19-year-old scored 39 on debut and while coach Andy Richards believed Barty had the potential to represent Australia's cricket team she returned to tennis after the season finished.

PLAYER'S VERDICT

Brisbane Heat all-rounder Jess Jonassen will long remember being out in the middle when a piece of WBBL history was made.

What was your magic moment from WBBL|01?

Grace Harris's 103 against the Sydney Sixers was very special because it was the first century scored in the WBBL and I was fortunate enough to be out in the middle when she did it. It's something I'll always remember as magical.

Was the pressure in the WBBL more intense than anything you've experienced in the 50-over game?

It was intense in the sense of the scheduling because none of us were used to playing two games on the one day or four games in three days. It meant the match-day intensity was, in a sense, doubled. However, while it was tough it was also a very exciting time as well.

What did the Brisbane Heat learn from its first season in the WBBL?

We learnt the team's momentum needs to be powerful. Once we got our first win we continued for a little while but after we had a break [for Christmas] it was hard to get that back.

How do you develop that for WBBL|02?

We need consistency across the whole board. We need one of our top-five batters to bat deep into the innings so we can post a really competitive total, because the women's T20 game is reaching the 140-plus runs mark, and the Heat has the bowling stocks to defend that kind of figure.

Name the Heat's best player.

It's tough because Beth Mooney played with great consistency throughout the tournament [scoring 400 runs at 33.33, taking 11 catches and completing 5 stumpings]. However, the value Grace Harris brought to the team—scoring the first WBBL century and taking 13 wickets—along with her character, meant, for me, they finished equal best.

PREVIEW OF WBBL|02

THE DRAW

V SYDNEY SIXERS
Sydney,
11 & 12 December 2016

V PERTH SCORCHERS
Perth,
17 & 18 December 2016

V MELBOURNE STARS
Brisbane,
26 & 27 December 2016

V SYDNEY THUNDER
Sydney,
2 & 3 January 2017

V HOBART HURRICANES
Blundstone Arena,
8 & 9 January 2017

V MELBOURNE RENEGADES
Brisbane,
14 & 15 January 2017

V ADELAIDE STRIKERS
The Gabba,
20 & 21 January 2017

WBBL|02 SQUAD

Jemma Barsby, Deandra Dottin, Holly Ferling, Laura Harris, Courtney Hill, Kara Sutherland, Jess Jonassen, Delissa Kimmince, Beth Mooney
Coach: Andy Richards

THREE KEY PLAYERS

HOLLY FERLING

Bowler Holly Ferling was a few weeks short of her 14th birthday when she made her debut in men's grade cricket in Kingaroy, and she was good enough to take a hat-trick with the first three balls she bowled. Four years later she was in the thick of Australia's 2013 World Cup campaign, taking 9 wickets at an average of 10.55. Ferling was the Heat's first WBBL recruit, and the 20-year-old lived up to all expectations with a 4–8 against Perth among her 15-wicket haul. Facing up to Ferling at full cry in the nets helped prepare her brother Lane for a rough 'n' tumble rugby league career with Brisbane Norths.

DELISSA KIMMINCE

Delissa Kimmince evolved from a fast teenaged bowler to an exciting all-rounder who, like Glenn Maxwell, likes to improvise when she's batting, playing reverse sweeps and ramp shots. The 27-year-old was picked for the first of her 11 one-day internationals when she was only 18, and helped Australia fight back to win the Rose Bowl series against the Kiwis. She took a break from the game in 2009 to travel and explore career opportunities. Kimmince's favourite saying is from former South African president Nelson Mandela: 'Do not judge me by my successes, judge me by how many times I fell down and got back up again.'

BETH MOONEY

Former Australian keeper Jodie Fields handed over the gloves a few summers ago so Beth Mooney could push her claims for national selection, and the 22-year-old from Hervey Bay used WBBL|01 as a platform to gain selection in Australia's World T20 squad. Her performance with the bat—she amassed 400 runs—and good form behind the stumps didn't escape the Southern Stars' first-choice wicketkeeper, Alyssa Healy. She publicly acknowledged Mooney as a genuine threat by saying it was nice to have good competition. Mooney has also played in England for Yorkshire.

Getty Images

Ferling strikes: Jess Jonassen joins pace bowler Holly Ferling in celebrating the prized wicket of Perth's Nicole Bolton during their clash at Aquinas College.

WHAT'S IN STORE FOR THIS SEASON

BEST-CASE SCENARIO

That the Heat finds the momentum needed to break into the final four. Brisbane fought hard to secure their first win in WBBL|01, and while they enjoyed a five-match winning streak after that victory, they lost all cohesion following the Christmas break. Consequently the Heat lost touch with the competition's pace-setters and couldn't make up the lost ground in the scramble for the semi finals.

BIGGEST CHALLENGE

That someone fills the void left by Grace Harris after she accepted an offer to galvanise the Melbourne Renegades batting order. Harris was a big—and popular—personality at the Heat. Her contributions with the bat—the highlight of which was scoring the tournament's first century—was invaluable.

BRISBANE HEAT

THE GABBA

(Brisbane Cricket Ground)

ESTABLISHED
1895

CAPACITY
39,000

PLAYING AREA
170.6 × 149.9 m

FIRST BBL MATCH
BRISBANE HEAT V MELBOURNE STARS
(20 December 2011)

FIRST TEST
AUSTRALIA V SOUTH AFRICA
(1931)

It was at the Gabba in 1960 that Richie Benaud's Australians and Frank Worrell's West Indians featured in the first tied Test. It also witnessed scenes of jubilation in 1995, when Queensland broke a 69-year drought to clinch its inaugural Sheffield Shield title. A redevelopment in the 1980s saw the Moreton Bay fig trees, grassy banks and greyhound track replaced by first-class facilities for players and spectators. The normally fast and bouncy pitch allowed demon bowlers Dennis Lillee and Jeff Thomson to terrorise the English tourists during the 1974–75 Ashes series, and the home team hasn't lost a Test match there since 1988. Brisbane crowds love the excitement of the BBL, and the Heat enjoys a loyal following.

Getty Images

FOUNDED:	2015
COLOUR:	Purple
HOME GROUNDS:	Blundstone Arena, Aurora Stadium and Kingston Twin Ovals
GAME RESULTS WBBL|01:	**Wins:** 8 • **Losses:** 6
POSITION FINISHED WBBL|01:	Lost semi final; finished regular season second
MOST WBBL|01 RUNS:	Heather Knight 363 **HS:** 74 • **Av:** 24.20 • **S/R:** 92.36
MOST WBBL|01 WICKETS:	Veronica Pyke 22 **BBI:** 3–19 • **Av:** 13.09 • **Econ:** 5.53 • **S/R:** 14.1
MOST WBBL|01 CATCHES:	Erin Burns 9
WBBL|01 SQUAD:	Heather Knight (c), Erin Burns, Katelyn Fryett, Kim Garth, Corinne Hall, Brooke Hepburn, Julie Hunter, Hayley Matthews, Sasha Moloney, Meg Phillips, Veronica Pyke, Celeste Raack, Amy Satterthwaite, Emily Smith, Emma Thompson **Coach:** Julia Price
PLAYER OF THE YEAR:	Heather Knight

Whirlwinds: The unheralded Hobart Hurricanes were the surprise packet of the WBBL, defeating the competition's eventual champions the Sydney Thunder.

SEASON SNAPSHOT WBBL|01

The Julia Price-coached Hurricanes created history by becoming the first Tasmanian women's cricket team to qualify for the finals of a national competition. Unfortunately, rain played a role in preventing Hobart from going all the way to the final when the semi against the Sixers was reduced to 14 overs. That move favoured a Sydney team crammed with some of the competition's genuine power-hitters. While English import Heather Knight excelled with 363 runs and 17 wickets, the team's success was attributed to the work that was invested in developing a winning culture over the years, something which included ensuring that the core of Tasmania's players trained together during the off-season rather than repeating the traditional winter practice of players doing their 'own thing' on the mainland. The trust they'd fostered during their gruelling training sessions came to the fore as the likes of Corinne Hall, Heather Knight, Veronica Pyke, Erin Burns and Hayley Matthews turned the tournament's so-called underdogs into genuine title contenders.

PLAYER'S VERDICT

The Hobart Hurricanes were a cyclonic force in WBBL|01, but Corinne Hall could be forgiven for being unhappy with Mother Nature's role in the downfall.

Have you forgiven Mother Nature for your rain-affected finals loss to the Sydney Sixers?

Yes, absolutely. Any shortened format was always going to suit the Sixers more than us. It was a trend during our season where we tended to grind matches out, whereas they had power hitters like Alyssa Healy. While there may have been some ill feelings directed towards Mother Nature after the loss, we're all over it now.

The Hurricanes shocked plenty, coming from nowhere in the competition.

Having us all based in the one place built a great team spirit and a great culture. We went into the season believing we had nothing to lose, we were the underdogs.

What was the biggest lesson of WBBL|01?

We played our best cricket when we didn't worry about the outside influences. We tended to put a bit more pressure on ourselves by listening to what was being said in the media. However, we'll learn from that next season when we're playing in pressure matches.

How will the Hurricanes handle the expectations for WBBL|02?

That will be a challenge. The pressure on us this summer will be a test. Our younger girls have learnt from the experience of playing against the best players in the world and from being led by one of the best in Heather Knight. She's taught us a lot. One important thing is we try to keep things simple and there are definitely no egos in our group.

Name Hobart's best player.

The veteran, Veronica Pyke. She's been around for a long time and has the respect of all the girls in the team. There are heavyweight fast bowlers in the competition but she just does her thing week in, week out. She was our best while Heather [Knight] contributed a lot with the bat and ball.

PREVIEW OF WBBL|02

THE DRAW

V PERTH SCORCHERS
Sydney, 10 & 11 December 2016

V MELBOURNE RENEGADES
Bendigo,
17 & 18 December 2016

V ADELAIDE STRIKERS
Adelaide,
26 & 27 December 2016

V SYDNEY SIXERS
Sydney, 29 December 2016

V SYDNEY THUNDER
Launceston, 5 January 2017

V BRISBANE HEAT
Blundstone Arena,
8 & 9 January 2017

V SYDNEY SIXERS
Sydney, 13 January 2017

V SYDNEY THUNDER
Blundstone Arena,
16 January 2017

V MELBOURNE STARS
Blundstone Arena,
20 & 21 January 2017

WBBL|02 SQUAD

Erin Burns, Katelyn Fryett, Corinne Hall, Brooke Hepburn, Julie Hunter, Heather Knight, Sasha Moloney, Meg Phillips, Veronica Pyke, Celeste Raack, Georgia Redmayne, Emma Thompson **Coach:** Julia Price

THREE KEY PLAYERS

ERIN BURNS

Erin Burns's playing career as an all-rounder was saved by revolutionary treatment from the Sydney Swans doctor Nathan Gibbs in 2014, when a cartilage tear resulted in bone on bone in her knee. She had a stem cell injection: stems cells were taken from her fat and injected into her knee with the intention of regenerating the cartilage surface. The procedure was a tremendous success. Burns is also an avid surfer, and last year she cycled from Sydney to Melbourne. She makes opposition bowlers fight for her wicket, and crowned her 224 WBBL runs with 7 wickets.

HEATHER KNIGHT

Heather Knight was the Hurricanes most dominant batter in WBBL|01 scoring an impressive 363 runs, while her 17 wickets meant she was the Tasmanian team's second highest wicket taker behind Veronica Pyke. However, her captaincy provided the Hurricanes—who almost qualified for the final—with an edge. That trait was enhanced during the English summer when she was named her national team's skipper following the retirement of Charlotte Edwards. Australian players are well aware of her mental toughness—she batted for seven hours against them in a 2013 Test to score 157, which secured a draw that helped regain the Ashes.

VERONICA PYKE

The veteran was at the forefront of the purple haze that enveloped the WBBL for most of the summer, taking 22 wickets at an enviable average of 13.09. Veronica Pyke's crafty bowling—her length-ball rattled a number of opposing batters—also ensured she finished WBBL|01 with a healthy economy rate of 5.53 runs per over. While pipped by Heather Knight for the Hurricanes' player of the year award, Pyke was viewed by many as Hobart's heart 'n' soul.

WHAT'S IN STORE FOR THIS SEASON

BEST-CASE SCENARIO

That Hobart picks up immediately from where they finished last season, especially with their sensational fielding. Their WBBL|01 season was derailed by Melbourne's big wet when rain forced their semi against the Sixers to become a shortened match. While it was a cruel blow, the Hurricanes proved they know how to win.

BIGGEST CHALLENGE

One is to forget last summer and start all over again, another is to realise they're now identified by rivals as a team to beat. The squad must also contend with the weight of expectation on them after the amount of local media coverage they generated during WBBL|01.

Getty Images

Competitive edge: English import Heather Knight finished WBBL|01 as Hobart's leading run scorer, but her leadership provided the tournament's surprise packet with an edge.

BLUNDSTONE ARENA

ESTABLISHED
1914

CAPACITY
19,500

PLAYING AREA
175 × 135 m

FIRST BBL MATCH
HOBART HURRICANES V SYDNEY SIXERS
(21 December 2011)

FIRST TEST
AUSTRALIA V SRI LANKA
(1989)

Football and cricket were first played on what is now Bellerive Oval in the mid-19th century, but the state's cricket headquarters was established at the Tasmanian Cricket Association ground in 1870. When Tasmania was admitted to the Sheffield Shield competition in 1977, Bellerive was upgraded with new grandstands, cricket nets, hill, surface, centre wicket and member's pavilion. It staged the state's first international match in 1988, when Sri Lanka played New Zealand in a one-dayer. A year later it hosted Tasmania's first Test, pitching an Australia team featuring local heroes David Boon and Greg Campbell against the Sri Lankans. Light towers were installed in 2009, and in 2013–14 the Ricky Ponting Stand was added, offering 5000 more seats.

Getty Images

MELBOURNE RENEGADES

FOUNDED:	2015
COLOUR:	Red
HOME GROUNDS:	Etihad Stadium and Junction Oval
GAME RESULTS WBBL|01:	**Wins:** 4 • **Losses:** 10
POSITION FINISHED WBBL|01:	Eighth
MOST WBBL|01 RUNS:	Dane van Niekerk 275 **HS:** 52 • **Av:** 19.64 • **S/R:** 99.27
MOST WBBL|01 WICKETS:	Molly Strano 18 **BBI:** 5–15 • **Av:** 16.72 • **Econ:** 6.12 • **S/R:** 16.30
MOST WBBL|01 CATCHES:	Sarah Elliott 8
WBBL|01 SQUAD:	Sarah Elliott (c), Briana Binch, Makinley Blows, Kris Britt, Cassie Brock, Nicola Hancock, Mariko Hill, Shabnim Ismail, Erica Kershaw, Kristy Lamb, Sophie Molineux, Rachel Priest, Molly Strano, Jenny Taffs, Dane van Niekerk, Georgia Wareham, Danielle Wyatt **Coach**: Lachlan Stevens
PLAYER OF THE YEAR:	Molly Strano

Young guns: The Melbourne Renegades fielded a youthful squad in WBBL|01, but the likes of Shabnim Ismail offered her team some solid direction.

SEASON SNAPSHOT WBBL|01

The Melbourne Renegades celebrated only four wins from their 14 matches, but two of them were on the biggest stage possible—live on Network Ten and in front of five-figured crowds at the grounds. A bumper 400,000 viewers tuned in as they beat the star-studded Stars in the Melbourne derby at the MCG while another huge television audience watched them upset the competition's eventual winners, the Sydney Thunder.
A stand-out performer was English all-rounder Danni Wyatt, who, at 24 was one of the Renegades' senior players. She added 14 scalps to her 249 runs. While the Renegades finished in last place, their season was haunted by a number of 'if only' moments, which included losing to Hobart on two occasions when they appeared on track for victory, a super-over defeat to the Strikers, an 8-run loss to the Stars, and falling to the Thunder in the final over.

PLAYER'S VERDICT

Molly Strano warns that the Renegades will be a better force thanks to the tough lessons of WBBL|01.

A hard year for the Renegades, but what did the team take from WBBL|01?

Managing only four wins and finishing on the bottom of the table was tough. However, we learnt it was about everyone chipping in during a game because when we won, it was the result of a few people putting their hands up instead of relying on our internationals or bigger names.

One great highlight must have been the crowds that turned out for the Melbourne derbies.

That was a thrill, because as female cricketers we're not really used to playing in front of big crowds. It was fun to play at the MCG before the men's derby and also at Etihad, where we had 14,000 spectators. They were two genuine highlights, and adding to those experiences was we won those games.

What did you get from playing in front of such large crowds?

It was a really good experience because before WBBL|01 I hadn't played in many televised games, and that certainly added pressure. The big lesson was to keep your composure because you can get nervous playing at the MCG and knowing the game was being televised. It was about keeping a clear mind and not allowing the external stuff to creep into your game and cramp your style.

How far off the pace-setters do you think the Renegades are ?

All the teams are even. We managed to beat the Sydney Thunder during the season, so that's a good indication of how close the competition is. It's really a matter of who brings their A-game on the day.

Who was the Renegade's best player?

Danni Wyatt chipped in with just on 250 runs, and she also took 14 wickets. I found she was also a barometer for us, because whenever she played well, the team did as well.

THE DRAW

V ADELAIDE STRIKERS
Sydney, 10 & 11 December 2016

V HOBART HURRICANES
Bendigo,
17 & 18 December 2016

V SYDNEY THUNDER
Sydney, 26 & 27 December 2016

V PERTH SCORCHERS
Etihad Stadium,
29 December 2016

V MELBOURNE STARS
MCG, 1 January 2017

V PERTH SCORCHERS
Melbourne,
4 January 2017

V MELBOURNE STARS
Etihad Stadium,
7 January 2017

V BRISBANE HEAT
Brisbane,
14 & 15 January 2017

V SYDNEY SIXERS
Sydney, 20 & 21 January 2017

WBBL|02 SQUAD

Kris Britt, Nicole Goodwin, Grace Harris, Shabnim Ismail, Kirsty Lamb, Sophie Molineux, Rachel Priest, Molly Strano, Tayla Vlaeminck, Georgia Wareham, Danielle Wyatt
Coach: Lachlan Stevens

PREVIEW OF WBBL|02

THREE KEY PLAYERS

GRACE HARRIS

The right-hander created history last summer when, playing for the Brisbane Heat, she needed only 52 balls to score the WBBL's first century and guide her team to its first victory of the tournament. The knock added to Grace Harris's growing reputation after she was earmarked as a player to watch following some impressive performances in the 2015 Ashes series. However, Harris made plenty of people smile after admitting she thought about 'ice cream' while she scored her historic ton. After convincing Harris to leave Brisbane, the Renegades are banking on her to replicate the 289 runs and 13 wickets she produced in WBBL|01.

MOLLY STRANO

Molly Strano has a huge supporter in Lisa Sthalekar, one of Australia's most respected female cricketers and a great spin bowler. Sthalekar wrote of her excitement when she saw Strano deliver the ball with what she described as a perfect seam position for an off spinner and, better still, from a height not often seen among Aussie spinners. Strano can't explain where her passion for cricket comes from; the 24-year-old's father was born in Italy and her mother was a dancer. Nevertheless, her reputation as one of the nation's best T20 players was enhanced by her 5–15 against the Stars.

SOPHIE MOLINEUX

This left-hander, who made her WBBL debut aged 17, is regarded as the next big thing in Victorian cricket. As a 16-year-old from Dandenong, Sophie Molineux was named Player of the Championships at the under-18 nationals after scoring 155 runs and taking 19 wickets. She also shined throughout the WBBL. Her 30 against the Stars helped guide the 'Gades to a victory, while she took 3–18 against the tournament's eventual champions, the Thunder. Her form captured the attention of the selectors, who picked her for the Governor-General's XI against India in 2016.

Teen queen: Sophie Molineux made her debut for the Renegades aged 17, but finished the summer earmarked as the next big thing of Victorian cricket.

WHAT'S IN STORE FOR THIS SEASON

BEST-CASE SCENARIO

That the Renegades win the moments that matter during their matches after last season's two close losses to Hobart; the 8-run loss to the Stars; losing to the Strikers in the super over; and falling to the Thunder in the final over. The Renegades did plenty of soul-searching and are certain to put their findings to good use during WBBL|02.

BIGGEST CHALLENGE

That their younger players don't leave it to the seniors to win games. The Renegades won only four games last summer but performed brilliantly whenever their games were televised by Network Ten. They must apply that same standard when the cameras aren't rolling. Someone must fill in for South African Dane van Niekerk who joined the Sixers as the 'Gade's leading runscorer.

MELBOURNE RENEGADES

ETIHAD STADIUM

ESTABLISHED
2000

CAPACITY
56,347

PLAYING AREA
170 × 140 m

FIRST BBL MATCH
MELBOURNE RENEGADES V PERTH SCORCHERS
(22 December 2011)

Etihad Stadium, one of the world's most technically advanced multipurpose sports and entertainment stadiums, was constructed for $460 million on wasteland. While the AFL relocated its headquarters there when the stadium opened in 2000, the ground has also hosted elite rugby league, rugby union and soccer matches. It has the largest retractable roof in the southern hemisphere, and the amphitheatre-like design allows patrons to feel as though they're on top of the action. Despite some criticism of the drop-in pitch, Etihad Stadium has been the scene of some tense BBL battles. In one of BBL|05's most memorable moments, the Renegades' West Indian import Chris Gayle went to town against the Adelaide Strikers and hammered a world-record-equalling 12-ball half-century.

Getty Images

FOUNDED:	2015
COLOUR:	Green
HOME GROUNDS:	Melbourne Cricket Ground and Junction Oval
GAME RESULTS WBBL|01:	**Wins:** 7 • **Losses:** 7
POSITION FINISHED WBBL|01:	Fifth
MOST WBBL|01 RUNS:	Meg Lanning 560 **HS:** 90 • **Av:** 56 • **S/R:** 113.82
MOST WBBL|01 WICKETS:	Morna Nielsen 18 **BBI:** 3–12 • **Av:** 11 • **Econ:** 5.21 • **S/R:** 12.6 Natalie Sciver 18 **BBI:** 2–9 • **Av:** 18.27 • **Econ:** 6.24 • **S/R:** 17.5
MOST WBBL|01 CATCHES:	Meg Lanning 7
WBBL|01 SQUAD:	Meg Lanning (c), Kelly Applebee, Lily Bardsley, Kristen Beams, Mignon du Preez, Kath Hempenstall, Emma Inglis, Hayley Jensen, Emma Kearney, Alana King, Anna Lanning, Katie Mack, Morna Nielsen, Natalie Sciver, Gemma Triscari **Coach:** David Hemp
PLAYER OF THE YEAR:	Meg Lanning

Getty Images

Star struck: The Melbourne Stars didn't make enough runs during the tournament but they did the job in the opening match of the league against the Brisbane Heat.

SEASON SNAPSHOT WBBL|01

Meg Lanning was named the inaugural best player of the WBBL tournament after she scored a phenomenal 560 runs—which included nine sixes and 47 boundaries— at an average of 56, but the David Hemp-coached Stars still fell short of a berth in the finals. The reality of the Stars summer was while Lanning conquered numerous bowling attacks, the other 13 batters who were used throughout the tournament only managed to score 962 runs between them. That meant Lanning scored one-third of her team's total runs. While the Stars' bowlers performed magnificently—Morna Nielsen and Natalie Sciver both took 18 wickets and Emma Kearney added aggression—the team paid a hefty price on the competition ladder for failing to share the runs, a point that was highlighted in the tight games the Melbourne Stars played in.

PLAYER'S VERDICT

Getty Images

The Melbourne Stars finished fifth, and their captain Meg Lanning recalled a season where she'd have swapped personal glory for team success.

The Stars finished fifth. What hurt your finals aspirations?

Our bowlers did a great job throughout most of the tournament but we didn't have enough depth in our batting to win a few of the close games we lost.

You scored 560 runs, did the Stars rely on you too much?

Obviously I want to score as many runs as I can, but in T20 cricket it's important to have multiple people contributing. That was an area where we lacked a little in WBBL|01, and it doesn't take much, maybe [a score of] 20 or 30, to make a difference.

What did being named the WBBL player of the tournament mean to you?

It was a huge honour, but I wanted team success first. It's nice when individual honours come along, especially in the first season of WBBL, because it was a massive step forward for women's cricket. As much as I'm proud of the award I want to see the Stars get into the final next year.

Will the pressure involved in WBBL matches improve women's cricket?

There were massive audiences watching when the games were televised on Network Ten, and that will add pressure to those big games—and that's what we're after. Women's cricket is in a good spot and we need to build on that in WBBL|02.

Which teammate impressed you?

Emma Kearney missed the first few games, but when she was given her chance through an injury [to a teammate] she did a tremendous job of opening the bowling for us.

Name your magic moment from WBBL|01.

The opening day of the WBBL, when we played Brisbane, the atmosphere was great and it meant a lot to see so many people were behind it.

PREVIEW OF WBBL|02

THE DRAW

V SYDNEY THUNDER
Sydney, 10 December 2016

V SYDNEY THUNDER
Albury, 13 December 2016

V SYDNEY SIXERS
Melbourne, 17 & 18 December 2016

V BRISBANE HEAT
Brisbane, 26 & 27 December 2016

V MELBOURNE RENEGADES
MCG, 1 January 2017

V PERTH SCORCHERS
Melbourne, 5 January 2017

V MELBOURNE RENEGADES
Etihad Stadium, 7 January 2017

V ADELAIDE STRIKERS
Melbourne, 10 January 2017

V ADELAIDE STRIKERS
Perth, 13 January 2017

V PERTH SCORCHERS
Perth, 15 January 2017

V HOBART HURRICANES
Blundstone Arena,
20 & 21 January 2017

WBBL|02 SQUAD

Meg Lanning (c), Lily Bardsley, Kristen Beams, Makinley Blows, Hayleigh Brennan, Jess Cameron, Emma Inglis, Hayley Jensen, Emma Kearney, Alana King, Anna Lanning, Katie Mack, Morna Nielsen, Natalie Sciver, Gemma Triscari **Coach:** David Hemp

THREE KEY PLAYERS

ANNA LANNING

Born two years to the day after her older sister Meg, 22-year-old Anna Lanning is making her mark as a batter in Victorian cricket. She's won the Una Paisley Medal, the prize presented to the most valuable player in the Victorian Women's Premier Competition, and played in 11 matches for the Stars in the inaugural WBBL competition. She says having the famous Lanning surname doesn't consume her, but she is determined to make a name for herself. After playing hundreds of backyard Tests, Lanning played her first game of club cricket when she was in primary school and Meg's team was short of players.

KATIE MACK

She was once famous for her leg spin and wild hairstyle, but Katie Mack has developed into an outstanding opener who forged a great partnership with Meg Lanning in WBBL|01, finishing second to her skipper on the run-scoring list, with 219 runs. The 23-year-old all-rounder, who in 2015 represented Australia's development team the Shooting Stars against England in Dubai, isn't scared to throw herself into her fielding, as her five catches for the Stars bear testimony. This health science student started her career with the NSW Breakers before moving to the ACT Meteors for greater opportunities.

EMMA INGLIS

Apart from being one of only four Victorian women to have played more than 100 matches for the state, Emma Inglis entered the record books as the first female general manager of the Melbourne University Cricket Club, which was established in 1856. Inglis, who has a bachelor of biomedical science degree, wanted more students to play the game and has allowed female students to realise there are greater opportunities available for them in cricket during this age of Ashes tours, World Cups and WBBL-style tournaments around the world. She enjoyed a tremendous debut season for the Stars, taking five catches and using her lightning-quick reflexes to complete 11 stumpings.

WHAT'S IN STORE FOR THIS SEASON

BEST-CASE SCENARIO

That the batting line-up packs greater depth this season. The Stars first showing in the WBBL was a one woman show with Australian skipper Meg Lanning scoring 560 runs—over a third of her team's total—setting up wins and being named player of the match in six of her team's seven victories.

THE CHALLENGE

For more batters to dig in and support their bowlers who did a great job. Lanning also can't be relied upon to make all of her team's runs. While the Stars led the table on the back of Lanning's season opening efforts gave them a 4–0 win record, when the lack of batting depth was exposed they tumbled from first to fifth and never recovered.

Mack attack: A one-time leg spinner with a wild hairstyle, Katie Mack has transformed into a solid opener who offered Meg Lanning some support in WBBL|01.

THE MELBOURNE CRICKET GROUND

ESTABLISHED
1853

CAPACITY
100,024

PLAYING AREA
172.9 × 147.8 m

FIRST BBL MATCH
MELBOURNE STARS V SYDNEY THUNDER
(17 December 2011)

FIRST TEST
AUSTRALIA V ENGLAND
(1877)

The MCG, the world's 10th largest stadium, has hosted the 1956 Summer Olympics, the 2006 Commonwealth Games and two ICC World Cup finals, and is the 'spiritual home' of Aussie Rules football. It was also the venue for the world's first cricket Test match, when Australia played England in 1877. In 1971, cricket's first one-day international was played there, Australia defeating England in a 40-over match. Until the 1970s, more than 120,000 people frequently crammed into the venue, but grandstand redevelopments and safety legislation have limited total capacity to 100,024. During BBL|05, world cricket bosses were forced to sit up and recognise T20's impact when more than 80,000 people turned out to watch the Melbourne derby between the Stars and Renegades.

Getty Images

PERTH SCORCHERS

FOUNDED:	2015
COLOUR:	Orange
HOME GROUNDS:	#TheFurnace (the WACA Ground) and Aquinas College, Perth
GAME RESULTS WBBL|01:	**Wins:** 7 • **Losses:** 7
POSITION FINISHED WBBL|01:	Lost semi final; finished regular season fourth
MOST WBBL|01 RUNS:	Charlotte Edwards 462 **HS:** 88* • **Av:** 42 • **S/R:** 103.58
MOST WBBL|01 WICKETS:	Katherine Brunt 16 **BBI:** 4–17 • **Av:** 17.12 • **Econ:** 5.02 • **S/R:** 20.4 Nicky Shaw 16 **BBI:** 3–28 • **Av:** 20 • **Econ:** 5.61 • **S/R:** 21.3
MOST WBBL|01 CATCHES:	Elyse Villani 8
WBBL|01 SQUAD:	Nicole Bolton (c), Meg Banting, Suzie Bates, Emma Biss, Katherine Brunt, Jess Cameron, Piepa Cleary, Laura Delany, Deandra Dottin, Charlotte Edwards, Heather Graham, Katie-Jane Hartshorn, Emma King, Chloe Piparo, Nicky Shaw, Elyse Villani, Jenny Wallace **Coach:** Lisa Keightley
PLAYER OF THE YEAR:	Katherine Brunt

Scorched Perth policy: Perth struggled to find consistency over the summer, but on their day they were one of the WBBL's most dangerous teams.

SEASON SNAPSHOT WBBL|01

English women Nicky Shaw and Katherine Brunt added plenty of fire 'n' brimstone to Perth's attack when they were called upon to open the bowling in each of their team's matches—and their efforts to capture 16 wickets each were described as 'restricting, relentless and ruthless'. They also provided the Scorchers batters with a platform to build on, with statistics noting that in six of their seven regular season victories the Scorchers won when they batted second. Charlotte Edwards, yet another English import, finished WBBL|01 as the tournament's second highest run-scorer with 462 runs, adding to her efforts was she carried her bat through on four occasions. While the Scorchers missed out on a berth in the title decider at the MCG, the efforts of Katie Hartshorn, Elyse Villani, Suzie Bates and Heather Graham ensured that on their day Perth has the potential to be one of the competition's danger teams.

PLAYER'S VERDICT

Elyse Villani says the Perth Scorchers won't allow stage fright to disrupt their WBBL|02 campaign.

What do the Scorchers think about when they reflect on WBBL|01?

The Scorchers learnt that we need to play a more consistent brand of cricket to be even more successful in WBBL|02. We're also hoping to put our best performances on television this summer, because we unfortunately bombed out there last season.

The schedule was tough for all teams, but did travelling from Perth make it even harder?

It wasn't ideal, but for the first year of competition we wanted to play as many games as possible. I think, given the choice between a hectic schedule or playing fewer games, everyone would have accepted that it was much better to play more matches.

Did you feel as though Perth supporters embraced their women's team?

Absolutely! If you head out to #TheFurnace on match day, it's always packed and has a great atmosphere. We were lucky the fans embraced us and that they see the Scorchers as one franchise and two teams. It's so incredible to be a part of that.

What was your magic moment from WBBL|01?

Making the semi finals was special because there was one stage when we weren't sure whether that would happen. However, we trained the house down over a two-week break and had two dominant wins over the Renegades to make the semi finals. I'd nominate that big turnaround as our magic moment.

Who was the Scorchers best player of the year?

Katherine Brunt won our award as the best player of the year and she deserved it because of her consistency. She regularly took wickets for us in the opening six overs, and it was a welcome habit—and she helped us gain momentum. The surprise packet of the summer was Katie Hartshorn with her left-arm off spin. I have no doubt she's only going to get bigger and better.

PREVIEW OF WBBL|02

THE DRAW

V HOBART HURRICANES
Sydney, 10 & 11 December 2016

V BRISBANE HEAT
Perth, 17 & 18 December 2016

V MELBOURNE RENEGADES
Etihad Stadium,
29 December 2016

V ADELAIDE STRIKERS
Adelaide Oval, 31 December 2016

V MELBOURNE RENEGADES
Melbourne, 4 January 2017

V MELBOURNE STARS
Melbourne, 5 January 2017

V SYDNEY SIXERS
Sydney, 8 & 9 January 2017

V ADELAIDE STRIKERS
#TheFurnace, 14 January 2017

V MELBOURNE STARS
Perth, 15 January 2017

V SYDNEY THUNDER
Perth, 20 & 21 January 201

WBBL|02 SQUAD

Nicole Bolton (c), Meg Banting, Suzie Bates, Emma Biss, Katherine Brunt, Mathilda Carmichael, Piepa Cleary, Lauren Ebsary, Heather Graham, Katie Hartshorn, Emma King, Chloe Piparo, Anya Shrubsole, Elyse Villani
Coach: Lisa Keightley

THREE KEY PLAYERS

SUZIE BATES

Beijing Olympian Suzie Bates received a huge accolade after WBBL|01 when she was named Wisden's Leading Women's Cricketer of the World. The Bible of cricket said the New Zealander's power-hitting—which included a double century against Sri Lanka and a one-day international century against England—meant she deserved the title. Just as Ellyse Perry worked hard to represent her nation in two sports, Bates once juggled basketball and cricket commitments. The highlight of her hoops career was being selected for the Tall Ferns at the Beijing summer Olympics. The 29-year-old, who has been New Zealand's permanent captain since 2012, will again add authority to the Scorchers.

NICOLE BOLTON

The left-hander heralded her arrival as an Australian international when she struck 124 runs against England in a one-day international at the MCG in 2014. Nicole Bolton earned her national spurs after gaining the reputation as one of the WNCL's most consistent batters, boasting over 1000 domestic runs when she took strike against England. After a one-season stint in Victoria, the 27-year-old returned to Perth to help lead the Scorchers' WBBL|01 campaign. Bolton has thrown her full support behind the charity Livin—which encourages people with mental health issues such as Depression to seek help—and raised money for the group by running in the 2016 City to Surf race in Sydney.

MATHILDA CARMICHAEL

After a dominant season for Melville in Western Australia's Female A grade competition, Mathilda Carmichael, a Hockeyroo, was signed to play for the Scorchers in WBBL|02. Carmichael, drew plenty of attention from Perth officials after she scored 337 runs at an average of 56 in her six games for Melville. After missing selection for the Rio de Janeiro Olympics, Carmichael decided to try and combine the two sports, revealing she still harbours aspirations to represent the Hockeyroos. The 22-year-old planned to compete in the Australian National (hockey) League.

Getty Images

Bolton-ing home: Perth batter Nicole Bolton proved her class when she made a stylish 124 against England in her one-day international debut at the MCG in 2014.

WHAT'S IN STORE FOR THIS SEASON

BEST-CASE SCENARIO

That the Scorchers forget last season; win more than two games in a row; and win more matches when they're sent into bat first. The Scorchers can't find themselves in the same position as WBBL|01 when they were scrambling for the last berth in the top four, all because they lacked momentum throughout the season.

THE CHALLENGE

For the planets to get into alignment early in the season. Charlotte Edwards scored a total of 462 runs; Ellyse Villani 326 and Suzie Bates a whirlwind 220 runs from her eight outings but, after that, runs from the rest of the squad were scarce. Perth's challenge is for other batters to share the load.

PERTH SCORCHERS

#THEFURNACE

Western Australia Cricket Association Ground (WACA)

ESTABLISHED
1893

CAPACITY
22,000

PLAYING AREA
149 × 139 m

FIRST BBL MATCH
PERTH SCORCHERS V HOBART HURRICANES
(18 December 2011)

FIRST TEST
AUSTRALIA V ENGLAND
(1970)

The WACA was opened in 1893, but the tyranny of distance made it difficult for Western Australia to host regular interstate matches before the Second World War, and it wasn't until 1947–48 that the 'Sandgropers' joined the Sheffield Shield competition. The WACA hosted its first Test during the 1970–71 Ashes series, where local heroes Rodney Marsh and Graham McKenzie starred. The ground is renowned for its fast bouncy wicket and the famous 'Fremantle Doctor', a breeze that sweeps along the Swan River and not only relieves the city of its stifling heat but also assists swing bowlers. Referred to as #TheFurnace by the Scorchers faithful during the BBL, it's considered one of the toughest grounds for visiting teams.

Getty Images

FOUNDED:	2015
COLOUR:	Magenta
HOME GROUNDS:	Sydney Cricket Ground, Waverly Oval and Drummoyne Oval
GAME RESULTS WBBL|01:	**Wins:** 8 • **Losses:** 6
POSITION FINISHED WBBL|01:	Runners-up; finished regular season third
MOST WBBL|01 RUNS:	Ellyse Perry 430 **HS:** 67* • **Av:** 33.07 • **S/R:** 94.29
MOST WBBL|01 WICKETS:	Sarah Aley 19 **BBI:** 4–8 • **Av:** 15.78 • **Econ:** 6.20 • **S/R:** 15.2
MOST WBBL|01 CATCHES:	Alyssa Healy 6
WBBL|01 SQUAD:	Ellyse Perry (c), Sarah Aley, Rhiannon Dick, Ashleigh Gardner, Alyssa Healy, Jodie Hicks, Sara Hungerford, Marizanne Kapp, Emily Leys, Sara McGlashan, Laura Marsh, Angela Reakes, Rachel Scholes, Lauren Smith, Lisa Sthalekar, Kara Sutherland **Coach:** Ben Sawyer
PLAYER OF THE YEAR:	Marizanne Kapp

Spinning out: The Sixers' Lisa Sthalekar is the centre of attention after dismissing the Thunder's Erin Osborne in Sydney's cross-city derby at the SCG.

SEASON SNAPSHOT WBBL|01

After a disastrous start in which the much-derided Sixers lost their opening six matches, they were charged, according to their coach Ben Sawyer, with a positive energy born of accepting they had nothing to lose in their run home. After the Christmas break, the Sixers won eight consecutive matches to earn their semi-final berth against the Hobart Hurricanes. They won their first match after the Christmas break, adopted the hashtag #SixersAreGoingVertical, made their way through to a rain-affected semi, then won the chance to challenge arch rivals the Thunder in the final at the MCG. The Sixers may have missed a podium finish, but their defiance of the odds has provided the outstanding foundation they need to build a strong team culture. While seasoned internationals Ellyse Perry (as captain), Alyssa Healy, Lisa Sthalekar, South Africa's Marizanne Kapp and Kiwi destroyer Sara McGlashan all excelled, teenager Ashleigh Gardner emerged as a star of the future.

PLAYER'S VERDICT

Sydney Sixers captain Ellyse Perry reflected on a season where her team needed to respond to numerous challenges.

What did the Sixers take from the final?

The fact we qualified for the final was a pretty special achievement after a tough start. Our season brought us very close together. We would have loved to have finished it off [with the trophy], but in terms of setting a platform for seasons to come—and seeing how much the girls improved—it was fitting that we made the final.

You must have been proud your team refused to give in after losing the first six matches of the season.

To make the final from that position was special, especially because some people had written us off. We didn't post enough runs against the Thunder [in the final] but to be still alive and kicking in the last over was a great effort.

What improvements do you want from the Sixers in WBBL|02?

Some more consistency—and earlier in the season—would be really nice! I'm very excited about WBBL|02, because I think we've started something really quite special. It's been a pleasure to play with the girls and to work with the coaching staff we've had, and we can continue to forge our relationships.

Name the Sixers best player.

Across the whole season it was Marizanne Kapp. She was unbelievably reliable with the ball, and she set the tone for us. Her bowling reflected the way we want to play our cricket: very aggressively—she doesn't hold back. I think Ash Gardner deserves a special mention; she's a very young player but took on board batting at No. 3 and did a fantastic job.

What was your magic moment from WBBL|01?

Winning the last game of the regular round of the season against Hobart from what seemed to be at one stage an unwinnable position [the Sixers were 4–20]. Sara McGlashan's innings [79 not out from 58 balls] was incredible, and it was a huge highlight from a very special day.

PREVIEW OF WBBL|02

THE DRAW

V BRISBANE HEAT
Sydney, 11 & 12 December 2016

V MELBOURNE STARS
Melbourne,
17 & 18 December 2016

V SYDNEY THUNDER
Spotless Stadium
28 December 2016

V HOBART HURRICANES
Sydney, 29 December 2016

V ADELAIDE STRIKERS
Adelaide,
2 & 3 January 2017

V PERTH SCORCHERS
Sydney, 8 & 9 January 2017

V HOBART HURRICANES
Sydney, 13 January 2017

V SYDNEY THUNDER
SCG, 14 January 2017

V MELBOURNE RENEGADES
Sydney, 20 & 21 January 2017

WBBL|02 SQUAD

Ellyse Perry (c), Sarah Aley, Ashleigh Gardner, Alyssa Healy, Jodie Hicks, Haylee Hoffmeister, Marizanne Kapp, Carly Leeson, Emily Leys, Sara McGlashan, Angela Reakes, Lauren Smith, Lisa Sthalekar, Dane van Niekerk **Coach:** Ben Sawyer

THREE KEY PLAYERS

ALYSSA HEALY

Alyssa Healy boasts incredible cricket bloodlines: her father Greg was a member of the Queensland squad; her uncle Ian is regarded as Australia's greatest gloveman; while another uncle, Ken, played one first-class match for the Sunshine State. Her cousin Tom is also a keeper on the rise, being picked for the Australian under-19 team in 2015. After WBBL|01 Alyssa Healy married Mitchell Starc, the Australian men's fast bowler, announcing 'mine' on social media after their wedding ceremony. Healy is one of the genuine stars of women's world cricket and is Australia's first choice as keeper in each of the three formats. She's crucial if the Sixers are to go one better than last year's final.

ASHLEIGH GARDNER

Ashleigh Gardner, enjoyed an outstanding debut in WBBL|01. She nominates Andrew Symonds as the player who inspired her to try and knock the cover off the ball with big sixes and to bamboozle batters with her off spin. Gardner, who played her first game for the Sixers aged 18, showed incredible promise when she was 13 and made her debut for New South Wales in the Imparja Cup, an annual tournament for Indigenous cricketers played in Alice Springs. She has also won the prestigious Lord's Taverners Indigenous Player of the Year award.

MARIZANNE KAPP

The South African all-rounder was named the Sixers' best player last summer after she scored 152 runs and captured 17 wickets at an economy rate of 4.28 runs per over. Her outstanding tournament re-enforced she's one of only a handful of international players who are capable of opening both the batting and bowling. The 26-year-old shone during the WBBL|01 final against the Thunder when she top-scored for the Sixers with 21 and then took 1–7. Apart from competing in representative athletics, biathlon, lifesaving and netball, Kapp and fellow Sixers recruit Dane van Niekerk created history in South Africa by becoming the first female cricketers to train at the Eastern Province Cricket Academy.

WHAT'S IN STORE FOR THIS SEASON

BEST-CASE SCENARIO

That they can go one better and win the title. If the Sixers proved anything last summer it's they're a team blessed with a great spirit . . . a winning spirit . . . that complements their talent-rich squad. They stunned everyone by rallying from six consecutive defeats to win eight straight and meet the Thunder in the decider.

THE CHALLENGE

One is not to play the second half of the tournament under as much stress as they found themselves towards the end of last season! Another important test is that the team's impressive young talent, including 19-year-old Ashleigh Gardner, builds on the successes they enjoyed last season.

Getty Images

Top prospect: After an outstanding debut for the Sixers, teenager Ashleigh Gardner revealed as a child she was inspired to smash the ball like Andrew Symonds.

SYDNEY CRICKET GROUND

ESTABLISHED
1851

CAPACITY
48,000

PLAYING AREA
156 × 154 m

FIRST BBL MATCH
SYDNEY SIXERS V BRISBANE HEAT
(16 December 2011)

FIRST TEST
AUSTRALIA V ENGLAND
(1882)

Cricket has been played on the SCG site since 1851, when soldiers flattened the land and called it the Garrison Ground. In the ground's first Test match, in 1882, Australia defeated England by 5 wickets. The SCG is now considered a spin bowler's paradise, but the pitch earlier favoured batting; Don Bradman scored his unbeaten 452 against Queensland there in 1930. It's also witnessed 277 from West Indian Brian Lara in 1993, and Steve Waugh overcoming speculation about his Test future during the 2002–03 Ashes series by scoring a century off the last ball of Day 2. The heritage-listed Members' and Ladies' Pavilions are two famous landmarks, and the new Bradman, Noble and Messenger stands are internationally acclaimed.

Getty Images

FOUNDED:	2015
COLOUR:	Lime Green
HOME GROUNDS:	Spotless Stadium, Blacktown International Sportspark and Howell Oval
GAME RESULTS WBBL|01:	**Wins:** 11 • **Losses:** 5
POSITION FINISHED WBBL|01:	Champions; finished regular season first
MOST WBBL|01 RUNS:	Alex Blackwell 410 **HS:** 45 • **Av:** 45.55 • **S/R:** 101.23
MOST WBBL|01 WICKETS:	Rene Farrell 26 **BBI:** 4–18 • **Av:** 12.96 • **Econ:** 5.50 • **S/R:** 14.1
MOST WBBL|01 CATCHES:	Claire Koski 15
WBBL|01 SQUAD:	Alex Blackwell (c), Charlotte Anneveld, Samantha Bates, Nicola Carey, Lauren Cheatle, Stefanie Daffara, Rene Farrell, Maisy Gibson, Rachael Haynes, Mikayla Hinkley, Claire Koski, Erin Osborne, Naomi Stalenberg, Stafanie Taylor, Belinda Vakarewa **Coach:** Joanne Broadbent
PLAYER OF THE YEAR:	Stafanie Taylor

Thunder nation: The Sydney Thunder became the toast of the WBBL when they defeated their arch rivals, the Sixers, for the crown at the MCG.

SEASON SNAPSHOT WBBL|01

The Sydney Thunder didn't feature in many discussions when the experts predicted who'd win the inaugural WBBL title, but the squad coached by Joanne Broadbent made a compelling statement in its opening match. The women became the first team representing the Thunder ever to beat arch rivals the Sydney Sixers. While West Indies skipper Stafanie Taylor hammered an unconquered 59 from 38 deliveries at Penrith's Howell Oval, Alex Blackwell whacked an unbeaten 29 to allow her team to cruise to a 9-wicket victory. The Thunder's dominance wasn't reliant upon Blackwell and Taylor, two of international cricket's fiercest competitors. A number of consistent contributions throughout the 16-match campaign from teenage rookie Lauren Cheatle and Naomi Stalenberg, along with experienced campaigners including Rene Farrell and Rachael Haynes, guided the team to nine regular-season wins before they held their nerve to qualify for the semi final, then win the drama-charged final against the Sixers.

PLAYER'S VERDICT

Alex Blackwell, captain of the title-winning Sydney Thunder, reflected on a season during which her team defied the critics.

What did we learn about the Sydney Thunder in WBBL|01?

Everyone is a leader at the Thunder; it doesn't matter if it's your first game or 16th, you're there because you're considered good enough. We saw Maisy Gibson, for instance, take the ball as a young leg spinner and make an impact.

Describe what it meant to win the first WBBL competition.

We're determined to do it again. We had such a great time joining our men's team as the champions, and I'll never forget standing alongside Mike Hussey as we both held our team's trophies. We were underdogs; none of the critics mentioned us when they wrote their previews. It was nice, and it was exciting, to prove we were world-beaters, and we're hungry to do it again.

Can you pinpoint the reasons for the Thunder's success?

Everyone felt part of the team and the adventure we were on. Everyone realised they needed to contribute and we also communicated very well. After every game we used our debrief to discuss what we'd learnt, what we did well and we celebrated our small wins.

Name the Thunder's most valuable player.

A tough one, but Stafanie Taylor arrived as our international import from Jamaica and she brought her own style to the Thunder. She hit the ground running in our first game—the first ever Sydney bash—against the Sixers at Howell Oval in Penrith. Stafanie hit a huge six and it set the tone for the season.

What was your magic moment from WBBL|01?

To win the final and beat the Sixers for the title was awesome. To be champions alongside our men's team . . . it doesn't get any better than that. It's our goal to do it again, and I think what made it even more special was both teams flew under the radar.

PREVIEW OF WBBL|02

THE DRAW

V MELBOURNE STARS
Sydney, 10 & 13 December 2016

V MELBOURNE STARS
Albury, 13 December 2016

V ADELAIDE STRIKERS
Penrith, 16 & 17 December 2016

V MELBOURNE RENEGADES
Sydney, 26 & 27 December 2016

V SYDNEY SIXERS
Spotless Stadium,
28 December 2016

V BRISBANE HEAT
Sydney, 2 & 3 January 2017

V HOBART HURRICANES
Launceston, 5 January 2017

V SYDNEY SIXERS
SCG, 14 January 2017

V HOBART HURRICANES
Blundstone Arena, 16 January 2017

V PERTH SCORCHERS
Perth, 20 & 21 January 2017

WBBL|02 SQUAD

Alex Blackwell (c), Samantha Bates, Nicola Carey, Lauren Cheatle, Stefanie Daffara, Rene Farrell, Maisy Gibson, Rachael Haynes, Mikayla Hinkley, Harmanpreet Kaur, Claire Koski, Erin Osborne, Naomi Stalenberg, Stafanie Taylor, Belinda Vakarewa
Coach: Joanne Broadbent

THREE KEY PLAYERS

STAFANIE TAYLOR

When the West Indies skipper signed with the Thunder, the hard-hitting top-order batter Stafanie Taylor declared she'd be a 'huge asset' for her new team—and the 24-year-old lived up to her words. The all-rounder needed no time to establish herself as one of the competition's genuine entertainers, being named player of the match in her first appearance in the Sydney team's electric green battle colours. After helping guide the Thunder to the inaugural WBBL crown, the Jamaican then spearheaded the Windies to a shock win over Australia in the World T20 final. True to her Thunder-like form, Taylor was named best player in the ICC's tournament.

RENE FARRELL

The Thunder's first WBBL recruit and a member of the triumphant 2015 Ashes touring squad, Rene Farrell finished her campaign with 26 well-deserved wickets. Alex Blackwell describes the 29-year-old as a 'superstar', and few could disagree after her outstanding performances in the WBBL, the highlight of which was skittling the Melbourne Renegades with a masterful 4–18. Farrell also serves alongside the likes of former prime ministers John Howard and Julia Gillard as an ambassador for Soldier On, an organisation that raises awareness of the physical and psychological effects of warfare.

MAISY GIBSON

This talented leg spinner, who took 2–21 in the drama-charged title decider against the Sydney Sixers, is one of a number of super-talented youngsters in the Thunder's ranks. Maisy Gibson played alongside the squad's teen sensations Belinda Vakarewa, Lauren Cheatle and Mikayla Hinkley in the 2014–15 NSW Metropolitan team that won the under-18 national championships. Her resilience can't be questioned; she fought back bravely from two knee reconstructions to force her way into the NSW Youth Breakers team that toured Sri Lanka in 2015. In 2014–15 she became the first woman in Newcastle cricket's rich 120-year history to play in the men's first-grade competition.

Getty Images

Calypso flavour: The Thunder's Jamaican recruit Stafanie Taylor performed brilliantly to live up to her promise to be a 'huge asset' for her WBBL team.

WHAT'S IN STORE FOR THIS SEASON

BEST-CASE SCENARIO

It's quite simple, that the Thunder maintains the rage of WBBL|01 and defends their crown. It'll be important that the young bowlers who performed so brilliantly last summer—Lauren Cheatle, Belinda Vakarewa, Nicola Carey and Maisy Gibson—back up the impressive inroads they made along the way to winning the title.

THE CHALLENGE

Last season the Joanne Broadbent-coached Thunder started out as underdogs but they played a brand of cricket which—despite a few nervous hiccups towards the semi final—ensured they finished the regular season on top of the table. Other teams will have dissected what made the Thunder roar and the champions will need to counteract their plans.

SYDNEY THUNDER

SPOTLESS STADIUM

ESTABLISHED
1998

CAPACITY
24,000

PLAYING AREA
164 × 127.5 m

FIRST BBL MATCH
SYDNEY THUNDER V HOBART HURRICANES
(10 January 2015)

Situated within the Sydney Olympic Park precinct, Spotless Stadium has hosted rodeos, rock concerts, the Royal Easter Show's Grand Parade and the GWS Giants AFL team. Since 2015, when the Thunder relocated to Spotless from the nearby ANZ Stadium to play two home games, it's become the fortress for the BBL|05 champions. After an acclaimed $65 million upgrade completed in 2012, the stadium became a boutique venue providing up to 24,000 spectators with an intimate view of the game. One of the ground's highlights was Mike Hussey's emotion-charged final home game in 2016. The Melbourne Renegades formed a guard of honour when Hussey walked out to bat; he scored 13 from 12 deliveries before falling lbw to Dwayne Bravo.

Getty Images

BIG PERFORMERS

JAKE LEHMANN

BLAZING HIS OWN TRAIL

Jake Lehmann needed the first—and only—ball he faced against Hobart to fulfil every cricketer's secret fantasy: slogging a big six to secure his team, the Strikers, a BBL|05 home final.

When the then 23-year-old Lehmann, whose father Darren is the national team's coach, took strike in front of a massive Adelaide Oval crowd, his team needed 4 runs to win. 'When you grow up as a kid you dream of hitting a six off the last ball to win a final for your team,' said the batter with arguably cricket's best moustache since Merv Hughes. 'And to find myself in that situation in a BBL game—and to be able to do it—is something I'll remember forever.

'The funny thing is I was really nervous when I went out there, but once I got out into the middle, [my batting partner] Tim Ludeman was awesome. He spoke about the process—what to do and what to go through—and it came down to cricket and me backing my skills. We spoke about where [Simon] Milenko was going to bowl, and [the idea was] if he missed I was just going to have a go.'

Getty Images

Unlike those athletes who describe a significant moment in their career as seeming to unfold in slow motion, Lehmann remembers Milenko's ball coming towards him at lightning speed. 'It was "Here you go" and it was done,' he said of the six that sent Adelaide's fanatical supporters into a frenzy. 'It actually took me a few minutes to realise what had happened . . . it felt like it was just me and Lude out there . . . and when I looked around and saw there was 45,000 [people] it was such a great feeling.'

While Lehmann has said there were always higher expectations on him when he was a young cricketer because of his surname, his father continues to be a source of inspiration as he's progressing through the ranks. 'He's always been there for me, but more as a father than a cricket coach,' said Lehmann. 'While we love cricket, it's only a small part of our life. Dad has let me go down my own path, but if there was ever a reason for me to call someone [about a cricket issue] he'd definitely be the person I would call.'

ADELAIDE Strikers

BBL|05

BATTING

MATCHES:	5
INNINGS:	3
NOT OUTS:	1
RUNS:	44
HS:	24
AV:	22
BALLS FACED:	31
S/R:	141.93
SIXES:	1
FOURS:	4

FACT ATTACK

- Lehmann scored three Sheffield Shield centuries for South Australia in 2015–16, including 205 against Tasmania.
- While his father is Australia's national coach, Lehmann's uncle is former English Test cricketer Craig White.
- He was picked in the Australia A squad for the 2016 winter series against South Africa A.

RIGHT-ARM FAST-MEDIUM BOWLER

BEN LAUGHLIN

THE COMPETITIVE EDGE

BBL|05

BOWLING

MATCHES:	9
OVERS:	30
MAIDENS:	0
WICKETS:	12
RUNS:	242
BBI:	2–20
AV:	20.16
ECON:	8.06
S/R:	15

FACT ATTACK

- In 2013 Laughlin equalled the best figures in New Zealand's T20 competition by taking 6–28 for the Northern Knights against the Wellington Firebirds.
- He played two seasons in Scotland in his early 20s and says the expectation to perform as his team's foreign player taught him about responsibility.
- He was selected for the Australian one-day international and T20 teams one year after making his debut for Queensland.

Ben Laughlin loves the buzz, hype and family-friendly nature of the BBL, but the fast bowler is adamant the success of the competition is underpinned by a fierce competitiveness between rivals. With 60 wickets at an average of 19.66, Laughlin is the most successful bowler in BBL history, and during his stints with Adelaide and Hobart he's forged a reputation as one of the competition's best death bowlers.

'It feels as though the rivalries that existed between the states are breaking down with us playing together [in the BBL],' said Laughlin. 'But when we walk across the line to play we're all very competitive, we all have massive competitive streaks, and sometimes we lock horns . . . I think it adds to the entertainment for the crowd.'

Laughlin, a former one-day international and T20 bowler for Australia, said that while his role as a specialist limited-overs bowler didn't occur by design, he's proud every time he suits up in the Strikers' distinctive blue battle colours. 'It's just how things worked out. I always seemed to be there for the shorter format but just couldn't crack the red-ball stuff . . . I'd definitely love to still be playing first-class cricket. But T20 isn't a bad scene! I love the atmosphere. People come out in their thousands—there are thousands of kids in the crowd, which is healthy for the future of cricket—and there's a buzz about that time of the year. You go out as a player and enjoy the experience, and I think people can see from our body language that we're having fun.'

Laughlin, whose father Trevor played three Tests for Australia in 1978, said that while cricket may well be in his DNA, he never felt forced to follow his father's footsteps. 'I didn't really start playing until I was 13 or 14,' he said. 'Dad took me down to Wynnum Manly [in Brisbane] but I don't know if it was destiny . . . it just worked out that way, although I had some pretty good genes to help me. It wasn't until I was a little bit older, when I was in my 20s, that I [really talked to my father about his career], when I understood the game more and realised what it would take to be a professional cricketer—and we connected on a different level there.'

Getty Images

RIGHT-HAND BATSMAN/LEG-SPIN BOWLER

ADIL RASHID

JENNER'S LEGACY

Any disappointment Adil Rashid may have felt about being overlooked for the English Test team's tour of South Africa was quickly replaced by his 'wonderful experience' with the Adelaide Strikers—where his haul of 16 wickets made him a BBL danger man.

Rashid, a talented leg spinner and more than capable batter, joined his Yorkshire coach Jason Gillespie at the Strikers for BBL|05 after missing the plane to South Africa. Ironically, the form he's displayed since starring for Adelaide has made him a man in demand with the English selectors, a situation that could impact on the number of games he plays in this summer's BBL tournament.

It was Rashid's second stint in Adelaide after spending 2009 there as a T20 player alongside the likes of Nathan Lyon and Dan Cullen. While in the City of Churches, he trained under Terry Jenner, a former Test player who is perhaps better known in cricket history as the man who steered Shane Warne to greatness. When Jenner, who passed away in 2011, first spotted Rashid, he described the 14-year-old as an 'outrageous talent' and later hailed him as the greatest leg spin discovery since Warne.

Getty Images

During Rashid's season with the Strikers—where he captured 16 wickets, was named the BBL's second best player and picked in the team of the tournament—Rashid told the Adelaide media of Jenner's positive impact on him. 'He helped me a lot with my action and cricket brain,' said Rashid. 'I spent a lot of time with him in Australia and England. He was a big influence on me growing up.'

Upon his return to Yorkshire, Rashid described playing in BBL|05 as an eye opener: 'The Big Bash was a wonderful experience and I am really thankful to the Adelaide Strikers for giving me this opportunity. I feel as though it has improved my game immensely. Playing with crowds of over 50,000 viewers was a thrilling experience, and the ideal preparation for the one-day international series [against South Africa] and World T20. Playing against the world's best players enabled me to get the experience I required.'

While Rashid spoke highly of his Strikers teammates, saying they always had his back, his wicketkeeper, Tim Ludeman, confessed that opposing batsmen weren't the only ones who needed to be on their toes when the Englishman bowled. 'It's an experience, keeping to Adil with his variations,' he said. 'Nothing beats keeping to good-quality spinners, but obviously when the batters are struggling to pick someone like Adil you have your own struggles [as a keeper].'

BBL|05

BOWLING

MATCHES:	9
OVERS:	34.4
MAIDENS:	0
WICKETS:	16
RUNS:	226
BBI:	3–23
AV:	14.12
ECON:	6.51
S/R:	13

FACT ATTACK

- Rashid is the first player of Pakistani origin to represent Yorkshire.
- In his second Test he batted for four hours and almost saved the Test against Pakistan.
- Apart from Jenner, two other Aussies—Yorkshire's coach Jason Gillespie and England's coach Trevor Bayliss—have helped shape him into one of Test cricket's most exciting prospects.

LEFT-HAND BATSMAN/RIGHT-ARM OFFBREAK BOWLER

TRAVIS HEAD

MEMORIES OF HOOKESY

BBL|05

BATTING

MATCHES:	9
INNINGS:	9
NOT OUTS:	2
RUNS:	299
HS:	101*
AV:	42.71
BALLS FACED:	193
S/R:	154.92
SIXES:	20
FOURS:	17

BBL|05 BOWLING

OVERS:	13
MAIDENS:	0
WICKETS:	6
RUNS:	118
BBI:	3–16
AV:	19.66
ECON:	9.07
S/R:	13

FACT ATTACK

- Head became South Australia's youngest captain when he was given the honour aged 21.
- In 2015–16 he steered South Australia to its first Sheffield Shield final in 20 years.
- He made his international T20 debut against India on Australia Day 2016, scoring 2.

Getty Images

It was an innings that evoked memories of the incredible day in 1982 when David Hookes, one of South Australia's favourite sons, needed only 34 balls to score the nation's fastest-ever first-class hundred. While the late Hookes's century was born of his frustration that Victoria's declaration had made it impossible for South Australia to win their Sheffield Shield match at Adelaide Oval, Travis Head conceded his match-winning 101 not out from 53 balls against the Sixers on New Year's Eve came from feeling he needed to contribute.

The then 22-year-old may have been hailed 'the King of Adelaide' once he had bludgeoned 89 from the final 35 balls he faced—including 56 from the last 15—but before the match the pressure was on him to do something after scoring only 49 runs in his previous three BBL innings. 'I went through a stage at the start of the Sheffield Shield season, had an okay Matador Cup, then had a lean patch,' Head told *The Advertiser*. 'I looked at what I was doing on the training track and had a period of self-reflection and perhaps wasn't doing as much as I did last year. I got back in the nets and did sessions and continue the drills now—it's working.'

Head's efforts with the bat throughout BBL|05—there were 20 sixes among his haul of 299 runs—impressed plenty, including Craig Simmons, his teammate, who is one of only three batsmen in the league's history, alongside Usman Khawaja and Luke Wright, to have scored two centuries. 'I think the reason Travis managed to do what he did was all because he has such a simple game plan,' said Simmons. 'He's so still at the crease and he has no preconceived ideas. I think a lot of batsmen go in to bat targeting certain spots. However, he just possesses a unique ability to keep a very clear mind at the crease.'

Simmons agreed with the likes of Hookes's former teammate Wayne Phillips in describing Head's swashbuckling knock as unforgettable. 'It was unbelievable,' Simmons enthused. 'A hundred is a hundred, but when you're chasing a big score—we needed 50 off the last three overs—it was probably the best innings I've ever seen.'

RIGHT-HAND BATSMAN

CHRIS LYNN

FROM BACKYARD BRADMAN TO BBL BELTER

Had Chris Lynn's backyard in suburban Brisbane been a couple of metres longer and could accommodate the rugby league goalposts he badgered his father to construct, the BBL|05's 'King of the Six' could well be playing for the Brisbane Broncos NRL team alongside his junior footy teammate Ben Hunt.

Lynn, who cracked a stunning 27 sixes on his way to being named the player of last summer's tournament, remembers some of the best times of his childhood were spent in the backyard playing ferocious games of footy and cricket with his brothers, James and Matt. 'We used two palm trees as our goalposts, but because we didn't have room for real goalposts, Dad built a cricket net for us at the side of our house,' said Lynn.

'We even had a bowling machine, but we didn't use it often because we enjoyed that competitiveness you get from batting and bowling to each other. I was grateful Dad built that, because when I think about it there was a real satisfaction in going out into the backyard with my brothers and just playing. You see kids nowadays with their PlayStation or iPad and I want to say to them that the best years of your life are when you're a kid—and they pass quickly. They ought to make the most of them because they can play the PlayStations later on [in life].'

Getty Images

Last summer, Lynn enhanced his reputation as one of the most feared batters in the BBL in a series of destructive performances. The five consecutive sixes he belted off the Stars' former Test bowler Ben Hilfenhaus is considered one of the most amazing individual feats in the competition's history.

While he's represented the national T20 team with distinction, Lynn conceded it doesn't match his younger brother's army service in Afghanistan. Although he's renowned as a tough competitor, Lynn admits he unashamedly cried as he watched Matt's passing-out parade at the Enoggera Barracks in Brisbane. 'I've represented Australia in cricket, but Matty represents our country every day,' he said. 'Our servicemen don't get the accolades that athletes receive but they're amazing people. Obviously mum was nervous, but he's proud to serve. It takes a tough character to do what he does, but just as I don't see cricket as a job because I love it, he's exactly the same about the army.'

BRISBANE HEAT

BBL|05

BATTING

MATCHES:	8
INNINGS:	8
NOT OUTS:	1
RUNS:	378
HS:	101
AV:	54
BALLS FACED:	218
S/R:	173.39
SIXES:	27
FOURS:	23

FACT ATTACK

- Lynn's father Col represented Australia in water polo and he coached his son at school.
- While he's one of the shorter format's most destructive batsman, Lynn scored 250 in a 2015 Sheffield Shield match against Victoria.
- In his T20 international debut against England in 2014 he made 33 off 19 balls.

JOSH LALOR

BURYING DEMONS

BBL|05

BOWLING

MATCHES:	8
OVERS:	28
MAIDENS:	0
WICKETS:	4
RUNS:	204
BBI:	2–21
AV:	51
ECON:	7.28
S/R:	42

FACT ATTACK

- Lalor has a marketing degree from the University of Western Sydney and has worked in cricket administration.
- He made headlines in BBL|04 when he took a brilliant boundary catch, jumping the rope, to dismiss Stars skipper Cameron White. The catch was controversial but legal.
- Lalor is one of only a handful of Indigenous players who have represented New South Wales in first-class cricket.

When Josh Lalor dismissed Sydney Sixer Nathan Lyon to help the Brisbane Heat celebrate a drama-charged 6-run victory at the SCG, it also helped him put the past behind him.

Lalor's previous appearance at the grand old ground was in BBL|04, when he played for the Thunder against the Sixers. After bowling his first three overs he was in rare air, boasting 4–6 after mowing down the Sixers' star-studded top order. With the Sixers needing 23 off the final over for victory, Lalor appeared to have the man-of-the-match award stitched up, but then Jordan Silk unleashed his bat. He hit 15 off the first four deliveries, setting the scene for Steve O'Keefe to steal the victory with two consecutive boundaries. Lalor appeared mortified as he attempted to come to grips with the result.

A season later, after taking 1–26 in the Heat's victory over the Sixers—an effort that included 10 dot balls—he left the hallowed turf with his head held high. 'I managed to bury a few demons from the year before,' he said of the Heat's SCG triumph. 'I had an up-and-down game for the Thunder [back then], and it occurred to me later on if I'd bowled my four overs in reverse I would've been a hero and not the villain.

'I've never gone into Big Bash cricket with my eyes closed. I know that kind of thing is possible. It didn't work for me on that particular night, but when we were in a similar position for the Heat [the game went down to the last ball against the Sixers] we got across the line and it felt . . . nice.'

Lalor was signed by Heat coach Daniel Vettori to join fellow new recruits Andrew Fekete, Luke Feldman and Samuel Badree, to help freshen Brisbane's bowling attack. Vettori identified Lalor's left-arm angle—and his ability to swing the ball and tie the batsmen down at the end of an innings—as an asset the Heat needed.

While the Heat started their season slowly, Lalor suggests that Brisbane's resurgence towards the end of the tournament indicated the team is now poised to be one of the big improvers in BBL|06. 'We spent a lot of BBL|05 on the bottom of the ladder and I don't think that was an accurate reflection of the team we were,' he said. 'We were trying to figure each other out early on, and once we did that we won some games.'

LUKE FELDMAN

LAW AND ORDER

Luke Feldman recalled the most torturous experience of his cricket career not as seeing Hobart's Daniel Christian smash one of his deliveries a whopping 117 metres onto the Gabba's grandstand roof during BBL|05, but playing bush cricket against men when he was a boy.

Feldman, who was named the Sydney Sixers' best player in BBL|02, recalled the time when he was 13 and forced to bowl the 13th ball of an over for the Caboolture Snakes third-grade team after being called for a morale-crushing seventh wide. Legend suggests he sobbed as he walked back to his mark, after being punished by grizzled old-timers and not being able to hit the wicket.

While it might have seemed the end of the world at the time, Feldman, now a proud Queensland police officer, says his experiences against adults hardened him to become a first-class cricketer who has taken more than 140 wickets for his state and has represented the Hurricanes, Stars, Sixers, Thunder and Heat.

'When you're young and getting smashed around the park you learn to deal with it,' he said. 'You learn to form game plans, and it's really a good toughening-up process. A lot of guys who come through the cricket pathways are always the best juniors and the coaches tell them how good they are, but as a kid in men's cricket I was told how bad I was until I eventually got there.'

Perhaps his initiation into cricket was the reason Feldman could shrug off Christian taking the long handle to one of his deliveries in the only game he played during BBL|05. 'Make no mistake, that was a low point,' he said of Christian's whack. 'Earlier in the game I bowled Kumar Sangakkara and was really happy . . . then Dan came along. I had phone calls from friends to see if I was okay, and my answer was "It's the first time a ball has beaten me home!" '

Feldman, who once worked in the police service's intelligence section, monitoring and keeping road-toll statistics, says that job puts moments like being tonked out of the park into perspective. 'When you look at all the serious stuff in life this is just a game. Have a bowl and try to be successful,' he said. 'It keeps you grounded when you see people wrapped up in the little cricket bubble and they don't really see what's happening in the outside world.'

BRISBANE HEAT

BBL|04

BOWLING

MATCHES:	1
OVERS:	4
MAIDENS:	0
WICKETS:	1
RUNS:	53
BBI:	1–53
AV:	53
ECON:	13.25
S/R:	24

FACT ATTACK

- Feldman was discovered by Cricket Queensland after strong performances in the Townsville and Cairns club competitions.
- During his debut Sheffield Shield match against Victoria in Melbourne he made a citizen's arrest on someone who broke into his hotel room.
- He played for five different BBL teams in the competition's first five years.

NATHAN REARDON

SON OF THE OUTBACK

BBL|05

BATTING

MATCHES:	8
INNINGS:	8
NOT OUTS:	1
RUNS:	155
HS:	41
AV:	22.14
BALLS FACED:	137
S/R:	113. 13
SIXES:	5
FOURS:	9

FACT ATTACK

- Reardon played two T20 games for Australia under captain Aaron Finch against South Africa in 2014–15.
- His 147 for Queensland against the West Indies in 2009–10 included seven sixes.
- Away from cricket, fishing and the great outdoors Reardon has an interest in carpentry.

BRISBANE HEAT

While Nathan Reardon escaped the intensity of the BBL during the off-season by fishing in remote locations in the Gulf of Carpentaria, he also pushed his body to the point of exhaustion to help Queensland's drought-ravaged farmers. Reardon competed in the famous annual Julia Creek Dirt 'n' Dust Triathlon that's staged near Mount Isa and acknowledged by Olympians as one of Australia's most gruelling events. He finished footsore and tired, but raised $5000 for Aussie Helpers, a charity that helps 'fight poverty in the bush'.

A proud son of the Queensland outback, Reardon was raised in the Darling Downs township of Chinchilla before moving to Gladstone as a 13-year-old. He earned each and every dollar at Julia Creek as he swam 800 metres, rode his bike 25 kilometres and ran 5 kilometres under the unrelenting sun and against the unforgiving wind. 'The ride was really tough because you were in a 25 km/h headwind and up to a one-degree incline all the way into town.' Reardon said of the challenge he finished in an impressive one hour and 24 minutes. 'The temperature was 35 degrees, and while completing the triathlon wasn't easy, I was proud to do it.'

Reardon said he was motivated to do something to help the farmers. 'At the moment 96 per cent of Queensland is in drought and I thought the Julia Creek triathlon was a great way to raise money to help the farmers,' he said. 'Some might be battling depression; others could be struggling to put their kids through school.'

The left-hander, who has represented Australia in T20, recovered from his gruelling challenge by visiting untouched parts of Queensland's Gulf country. 'I grew up in a simple family and I have a fairly simple outlook on life,' he said. 'I enjoy the peace and quiet, and you get that in the outback, you get that in the boat.'

Getty Images

While casting a line a million miles from care, the 32-year-old had plenty to think about, including the intensity that typifies the BBL. 'No one goes out there to muck around anymore,' he said of facing many of the world's best bowlers. 'The hit 'n' giggle days are gone; it's been replaced by a mentality of wanting to win, and no one takes a backwards step. That's what makes it such a great competition.'

BEN DUNK

PREPARING FOR A SLAM DUNK

When Ben Dunk takes strike for the Hurricanes he'll be determined to tap back into the form that made him the BBL's most dangerous batter.

Dunk was BBL|03's leading run-scorer and his 395 runs—which included a rapid-fire 96—allowed him to join David Hussey, Aaron Finch, Jacques Kallis and Chris Lynn to hold the title as player of a BBL tournament.

That summer of runs also paved the North Queensland-born batter's way into Australia's T20 team and it also enticed the Mumbai Indians to recruit him to take on the IPL's star-studded bowling attacks.

However, the 29-year-old couldn't hide his frustrations when he admitted he'd batted well below his own expectations last summer when he managed to scrape together only 113 runs at an average of 14.12.

Getty Images

'BBL|04 was an average season and BBL|05 was below the standards I set myself,' he said.

'The weird thing about last summer was I felt as confident as I'd ever been. I averaged 60 in the Matador Cup, so I felt good. However, looking back I think that was probably the problem . . . maybe I took more risks that didn't come off because I was overly confident.'

Dunk plans to use BBL|06 to put the disappointments of the last two summers behind him and also to help the Hurricanes storm into the finals.

'It's been difficult to live up to BBL|03 but I'm looking forward to starting all over again and I'm sure if I can replicate that form it'll help Hobart as well,' he said.

'The great thing is once you do something [such as being named player of the tournament] you know you can get back . . . and that's the plan.'

As someone who grew up on a banana plantation Dunk isn't scared to put in the hard work needed to be ranked as one of the BBL's most brutal batters, saying the experiences of helping his parents made a lasting impression on him

'I realised I had a few options: do well at school, make it in cricket or prepare for a life on the farm . . . it only took a school holiday for me to knuckle down in the classroom and train hard in the nets!

'I like hard work, it's got me to where I am but working on the farm was something else! It was manual labour and you were out there regardless of the rain, the heat and the humidity.'

HOBART HURRICANES

BBL|05

BATTING

MATCHES:	8
INNINGS:	8
NOT OUTS:	0
RUNS:	113
HS:	37
AV:	14.12
BALLS FACED:	103
S/R:	109.70
SIXES:	2
FOURS:	10

FACT ATTACK

- Dunk was awarded a rugby and cricket scholarship at Brisbane Grammar School.
- In 2014 he became the first Australian to score a double century in the domestic competition when he scored 229 for Tasmania against Queensland.
- While he had a lean BBL|05 he amassed 837 Sheffield Shield runs in 2015–16.

LEFT-ARM MEDIUM-FAST BOWLER

SAM RAINBIRD

CROWD CONTROL

BBL|05

BOWLING

MATCHES:	6
OVERS:	20
MAIDENS:	0
WICKETS:	6
RUNS:	157
BBI:	3–37
AV:	26.16
ECON:	7.85
S/R:	20

FACT ATTACK

- Rainbird took 2 wickets in the National Performance Squad's shock win over Australia A in 2014.
- He nicknamed his pet rabbit Gulbis, claiming he frequently dismissed Evan Gulbis in the nets.
- He's a huge NBA fan and supports the Charlotte Hornets.

'He's a good young bowler; he bowled well.' With that, the then national skipper Michael Clarke introduced Sam Rainbird to the public after the left-arm fast bowler's extraordinary Sheffield Shield performance in 2013. The 21-year-old rookie took three of the biggest scalps in Australian cricket—Clarke, Steve Smith and David Warner—while playing for Tasmania against New South Wales in Sydney.

He finished his second Sheffield Shield appearance with 7–112, and gained much more than high praise from the likes of Clarke. 'That game provided me with the realisation I was good enough to do it,' said Rainbird. 'At state level, be it in first-class cricket or the Big Bash, you need that one performance. I've seen some very good cricketers who've never had that luck or breakthrough performance that they needed to believe in themselves, even though they should have had faith in their ability because they were good enough. I'm grateful that happened in my second [Shield] game, because it allowed me to believe I can get good players out.'

Rainbird admitted, however, that the biggest lesson from his first season of Big Bash cricket in BBL|05 was the need to cope with the pressure generated by the massive crowds that watch every move. He remembers his debut for the Hurricanes in their 95-run loss to the Sydney Sixers as a night when butterflies rioted in his stomach. 'I'd never played in front of a crowd like that, and I don't think I controlled my nerves as much as I would've liked.'

In that match he bowled 0–17 off two overs and was dismissed by Nathan Lyon for 1. 'I'd never played in front of so many people, and it says something to hear guys like Shaun Tait say they still get nervous in front of crowds that size. When I walked off the field [after my BBL debut] I thought, "It's just cricket: while it's the Big Bash I know what to do." '

Getty Images

Rainbird, who grew up near Blundstone Arena, says his T20 debut season also provided him with a greater understanding of the journey he's on. 'One of the great things about the BBL is the calibre of players in the competition,' he said. 'I'm playing alongside the likes of Kumar Sangakkara and Shaun Tait, two guys I've watched since I was 10. When you play against someone of Chris Gayle's calibre, you get a tremendous insight into the step up that would be needed for international cricket. I think that's why Australian cricket is doing well—the [BBL] crowds and the cricket is helping to develop players from a young age.'

SHAUN TAIT

DON'T DARE BLINK

At 32, Tait was selected for Australia's T20 national side after a series of impressive efforts during BBL|05, including the game when he destroyed the Thunder at Blundstone Arena.

Hurricanes fast bowler Jake Reed recalls Tait's opening spell in that game as so fast he couldn't afford to even blink—and he was a fielder! 'It was the first over of the innings, and Taity was steaming in to an in-form Shane Watson,' Reed recalled. 'He'd just dismissed Kallis, and the first ball to Watson reared up and hit his bat handle right on the money. He followed that up with a quick full outswinger that Watson edged to [wicketkeeper] Tim Paine. I was at fine leg admiring his work, but, at the same time, I was hoping the batsman didn't inside edge the ball, because I couldn't see the thing after Taity let go of it.'

Getty Images

While Tait admits he's 'getting on' as a speed demon, old-fashioned pride drove him to finish with the stunning 3–16 that set the Hurricanes up for victory over the Thunder. The former Adelaide Strikers spearhead told reporters how he reacted to finishing the previous match against Brisbane with 1–54. 'After the last game I had to go look in the mirror and come back well for the team,' he said. 'I'm getting on a bit, but I'm bowling well. T20 is one of those games where the more experienced players do well. It's a fast game. You've got to think about it a lot.'

Tait has played more than 150 T20 games, and Reed, who impressed with 6 wickets in three games, learnt all he could from the paceman known as the 'Wild Thing'. 'The main thing I learnt from Taity was his mindset as a fast bowler,' said Reed. 'Sometimes you go out and come off with 5 wickets, other times you get belted for 0–50. Shaun told me it's all part and parcel of cricket, and you just move on and prepare for the next game.'

While Reed spent hours seeking insights from Tait, he was shocked when asked if he ever padded up to face the Wild Thing at training to gain a different perspective on what makes him great. 'Mate, you wouldn't catch me strolling into big Taity's net,' he said, shaking his head. 'Leave that for the silly batsmen.'

HOBART HURRICANES

BBL|05

BOWLING

MATCHES:	8
OVERS:	31
MAIDENS:	0
WICKETS:	10
RUNS:	247
BBI:	3–16
AV:	24.70
ECON:	7.96
S/R:	18.6

FACT ATTACK

- Tait bowled the second-fastest delivery registered in cricket, a 161.1 km/h fireball.
- He took 23 wickets to help Australia win the 2007 World Cup.
- It had been so long since Tait played for Australia he didn't pick the phone up when selector Rod Marsh called to say he'd made the 2016 Aussie T20 team because he didn't recognise the number.

LEFT-HAND BATSMAN/WICKETKEEPER

KUMAR SANGAKKARA

EARLY MORNING INSPIRATION

BBL|05

BATTING

MATCHES:	8
INNINGS:	8
NOT OUTS:	0
RUNS:	105
HS:	43
AV:	13.12
BALLS FACED:	88
S/R:	119.31
SIXES:	2
FOURS:	8

FACT ATTACK

- Sangakkara was awarded the Ryde Gold Medal as the best all-round student at the prestigious Trinity College school in Kandy.
- Apart from being a member of his school's choir, Sangakkara also played the violin.
- He is second only to Don Bradman in posting the most Test scores in excess of 200.

While Kumar Sangakkara didn't live up to his normal lofty standards during his first stint for the Hurricanes, it's doubtful that he received an 'urgent' fax from his father in the early hours of the morning, as he occasionally did when a member of Sri Lanka's national team.

Sangakkara, who scored 12,400 runs at an average of 57.40 from his 134 Tests, scraped 105 runs together throughout BBL|05, and he didn't hide his frustration about failing to make the Blundstone Arena scoreboard tick over. 'You're picked to try and do a job for the side, and when you fail to do that in the sense of runs, that disappointment is there,' he said. 'I've tried to give everything I can, I have tried to prepare as well as I can but I haven't managed to convert it.'

Sangakkara told a group of schoolchildren on a popular Sri Lankan television show of those times over the years when his father tried to guide him through similar rough trots with pearls of wisdom—regardless of the hour. 'He has advice on everything for me. Whatever I do he has a tip,' Sangakkara said. 'I've been on tours and sometimes at two o'clock in the morning I get a phone call from someone in reception . . . South Africa, two in the morning . . . and they say, "There's an urgent fax from home."

'There I am thinking, "Maybe something serious has happened, but why would they fax if there is something serious, they'd probably call." The fax comes up and it's a page from either C.B. Fry's book on batting [published 1914] or Don Bradman's book on batting [published 1956] . . . a little page with a few lines . . . and my father has underlined those sentences saying, "Read this before you go out to bat tomorrow." '

Sangakkara, who'll return to Hobart for BBL|06, made it clear he loves the Apple Isle, and he extolled the virtues of his adopted state in a series of videos for Sri Lankan students he filmed in his role as an ambassador for the University of Tasmania. 'Twenty years from now, looking back, this will always be a special part of my life,' he said of playing for the Hurricanes. 'It will be one part of my life but a special part of it.'

Getty Images

CAMERON WHITE

IMPROVING WITH EVERY BALL

Cameron White finished a painstaking Sheffield Shield innings last summer certain that the lessons he'd learnt during his 332 minutes holding out against the NSW attack will help him when he turns out for the Melbourne Renegades during BBL|06.

White was under intense pressure to secure a draw and guide Victoria to the Sheffield Shield final. While the 32-year-old found sweating on each of the 253 deliveries akin to playing in a straitjacket, he has good reason to treasure the unconquered 97 with which he finished the game. 'It was satisfying because I've never been in a position to play like that, to play for a draw,' he recalled. 'That went against my nature, and it taught me that I can play more defensively—and it helped get us through to the Shield final. Looking back on it, I remember thinking, "Geez, I was a better player at the end of the day than when I started," because I'd learnt a lot about myself.

'Nathan Lyon, a great bowler, was bowling for the Blues, and there was one stage when all of the fielders were crowded around the bat. There was a lot of space in the outfield at the time, but I couldn't afford to take any risk. I needed to play a certain way.'

Getty Images

While the Sheffield Shield and BBL are worlds apart in terms of tactics and time, White said that long innings under the sun will add something extra to his BBL arsenal. 'It reinforced the importance of your mindset and the need to believe in it,' he said. 'And that applies to T20 cricket.'

White, who was a foundation player for the Melbourne Stars, is preparing for his second season in the Renegades' red battle colours. He's determined to help steer the team to its most successful season since BBL|02, when it finished the regular season in first place. 'I don't think there's a lot of work to be done to improve,' he said of the franchise that finished BBL|05 one spot outside of the top four. Obviously you need to improve every year or you'll be left behind, but I don't think we were that far off in BBL|05 and it certainly had nothing to do with our game plan. It's about executing and playing better, and I have no doubt that's what we'll be trying to do.'

MELBOURNE RENEGADES

BBL|05

BATTING

MATCHES:	8
INNINGS:	8
NOT OUTS:	1
RUNS:	235
HS:	61
AV:	33.57
BALLS FACED:	197
S/R:	119.28
SIXES:	9
FOURS:	18

FACT ATTACK

- White captained Victoria when he was only 20 years old.
- The great Indian batsman Sachin Tendulkar was White's first Test victim, caught by Michael Clarke.
- He's determined to force his way back into the national system, saying the success of Adam Voges proves the selectors don't see 30 as a barrier.

RIGHT-HAND BATSMAN

TOM COOPER

DUTCH COURAGE

BBL|05

BATTING

MATCHES:	8
INNINGS:	5
NOT OUTS:	1
RUNS:	39
HS:	25
AV:	9.75
BALLS FACED:	28
S/R:	139.28
SIXES:	1
FOURS:	4

FACT ATTACK

- Cooper scored 104 for Australia against South Africa at the 2005–06 World Youth Cup.
- His brother Ben was the Netherland's leading run-scorer in the qualifying matches for the last World T20, with 241 runs.
- Tom Cooper scored 203 not out against New South Wales in a 2011 Sheffield Shield match.

While the Melbourne Renegades' rosters have included a host of international players since BBL|01, none matches Tom Cooper's rise and rise from Aussie bush cricketer to fully fledged Dutch international. Wollongong born but Lismore raised, Cooper qualified to represent the Netherlands at World T20 and 50-over cups because his mother was born in Dutch New Guinea (now part of Indonesia)—and because of his unmistakable talent with the bat.

While the former Australia under-19 player is proud to wear the orange battle colours that represent his mother's heritage, he admitted to an occasional twinge of mixed feelings about his international allegiance. 'I'm very fortunate to have the honour of playing for the Netherlands,' said Cooper. 'I've travelled here, there and everywhere; I've played in some amazing cricket tournaments and I've also met some great people. However, it's always a funny one when people ask me about playing for the Netherlands or Australia, because in an ideal world I'd obviously love to represent Australia—we grow up here wanting to wear the baggy green Test cap. In saying that, the opportunities I've received through the Netherlands definitely mean a lot to me.'

Upon being selected for the Dutch national team in 2010, Cooper created history by becoming the first player to score half-centuries in each of his first three one-day internationals. Among his most notable feats as an international was being Holland's rock during the 2011 World Cup match against the West Indies, scoring an unbeaten 55 as his team was skittled for 115; finishing that tournament as the Netherland's second-highest run-scorer; and helping guide his adopted nation to a 6-wicket win over Scotland with an accomplished 80 at Rotterdam.

Getty Images

He's determined to produce similar performances for the Renegades throughout BBL|06, although he concedes the results of the Melbourne-based team have been inconsistent since finishing the regular BBL|02 season on top of the ladder. 'Our performances have been up and down since then, and that's been frustrating,' he said. 'However, playing for the Renegades has been a tremendous journey for me. I love pulling on the jersey; we have great fans, and off the field we're leaders in things like memberships.

'The players are looked after very well. From what I understand, we get looked after better than other teams. However, the reality is we've underperformed, and there's definitely a determination to change that this summer.'

NATHAN RIMMINGTON

AN APPETITE FOR SUCCESS

While most players know how to train for a high-octane BBL match, Melbourne Renegades medium-fast bowler Nathan Rimmington is fascinated by how to fuel his body to achieve its optimum potential.

Rimmington, who completed his Health Science diploma, speaks about the positive outcomes an effective nutrition management can have for an elite athlete with the same gusto as bowling the 'death' overs for the Renegades.

'I'm interested in eating the right foods for recovery and preparation,' said Rimmington, who, in 2007, became the first Australian to take a domestic T20 hat-trick when he played for Queensland. 'When I became a professional cricketer I didn't know too much about eating well and preparing myself, I was pretty naive.'

Rimmington follows a match day eating plan that's aimed to help him perform in the evening. 'I tend to get quite nervous throughout the [match] day, so I tend not to have a massive meal,' he said. 'I try and stagger my meals throughout the day but it's nothing too out there because in BBL you don't bowl 25 overs like you do in Sheffield Shield cricket.

'Breakfast is porridge or muesli and I'll have some sushi for lunch. I've found you need to get your timing right for the BBL because you start playing at 7 or 7.30pm, a time when you'd normally be eating dinner.

'I've been lucky over the last few years in that my meal times have been pushed back to 5pm because we have young children—and that's not a bad time to eat for the Big Bash. I'll have a sandwich or something light. We normally have a meal after the game to get our protein up and that could be pasta, some meat or perhaps a protein shake.'

Rimmington is desperate for a change of fortune this summer after battling through BBL|05 with a shoulder problem and BBL|04 with a broken toe.

The Western Australian-based bowler has proven his resilience over the years: apart from battling those ailments to play for the 'Gades, he returned from a hip injury eight years ago for which the cure included having the bone shaved.

'That was a time when Queensland had seven or eight good bowlers and I think I subconsciously felt as though I was making up the numbers,' he said. 'That injury was a big turning point . . . I didn't want to return and just make up the numbers . . . I wanted to contribute and be professional in everything I did.'

Getty Images

MELBOURNE RENEGADES

BBL|05

BOWLING	
MATCHES:	7
OVERS:	27
MAIDENS:	0
WICKETS:	7
RUNS:	225
BBI:	4–26
AV:	32.14
ECON:	8.33
S/R:	23.1

FACT ATTACK

- Rimmington didn't play his first game of outdoor cricket until he was 15, before that he was an enthusiastic indoor cricketer, playing alongside his father and sister.
- His sister Rikki-Lee represented Queensland in the WNCL and she also played for Australia's under-19 team.
- Apart from his T20 hat-trick, he took another one for Queensland against Western Australia in a 2009 limited overs match.

CHRIS TREMAIN

OPPORTUNITY KNOCKED

BBL|05

BOWLING

MATCHES:	8
OVERS:	32
MAIDENS:	1
WICKETS:	6
RUNS:	249
BBI:	2–48
AV:	41.50
ECON:	7.78
S/R:	32

FACT ATTACK

- Tremain grew up in Yeoval in the Central West of New South Wales, which is where bush poet Banjo Paterson, of 'Waltzing Matilda' fame, spent his first five years.
- He had a synthetic pitch on the family farm.
- His mother taught at his school and once sent him to the principal for mucking up in drama.

When Chris Tremain was offered the chance to play for Victoria in 2014, the first thing he needed to change was his mindset about having to nail down a permanent first-class berth while he was at New South Wales. Tremain took 18 wickets in the six games he played for New South Wales, but he realised it was going to be difficult to get a regular game when players of Pat Cummins's calibre were named 12th man.

The 25-year-old revealed that when he unpacked his bags after relocating to Melbourne, he also released the pressure that drove him in Sydney. 'It played a bit in my head,' he said of his determination to play more games for his home state. 'Whenever I was given the chance to play, the first thing I thought if I bowled a bad over was I'd be dropped and never play again because so many people were waiting in line. When I moved to Victoria, I made the conscious decision that if I played first-class cricket, club cricket or whatever I'd just enjoy it. That attitude helped. I stopped worrying about selections and made sure I did what was needed to be picked.'

Tremain stressed, however, that he'd never felt hard done by or that the selectors should have picked him ahead of anyone else named in his native state's bowling attack. 'I consider it such a privilege to wear the Victorian cap,' he said. 'I certainly don't harbour any ill feeling towards New South Wales for not having any opportunity for me, because all that meant was someone else had been given their shot. Never in a million years would I ever say, "I should play in front of that person," because that opportunity is theirs. I realised I just needed to find my opportunity.'

Tremain was rewarded for his tremendous form and effort throughout 2015–16 by being named in the Australia A squad. Now, the former Sydney Thunder representative wants to help the Renegades fulfil its potential. 'The Thunder had some of the best players and every year we seemed to promise the world and delivered an atlas,' he said. 'Every year I felt excited about the Thunder and I had the same feeling about the Renegades.

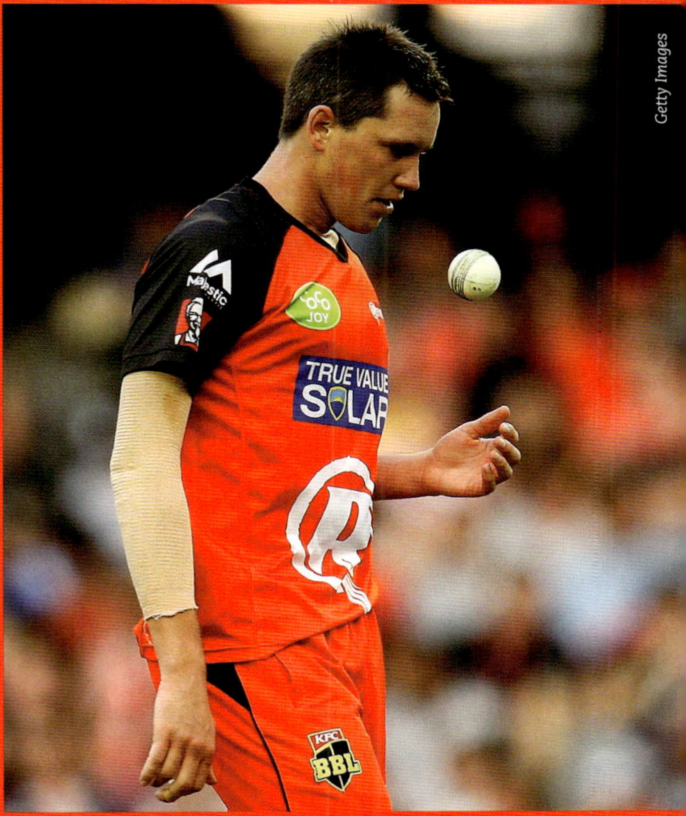

Getty Images

'You look at our squad and say wow, but we just need to click and form a winning habit. A winning habit is the same as a losing habit: when you're a frontrunner you seem to always be able to win from any position, and when you're struggling you can lose from any position—that's what the Thunder had for three years, but they won the competition in BBL|05.'

ADAM ZAMPA

ACCIDENTAL ACTION HERO

Adam Zampa is the BBL's answer to an accidental Hollywood action hero, a player who seems to be dragged into the thick of the drama whether he likes it or not. During BBL|05—his debut season for the Melbourne Stars—Zampa used his nose to run out the Renegades batter Peter Nevill! In BBL|04 he won a heart-stopper of a match for the Adelaide Strikers against Perth when, coming in to bat at No. 10, he blasted a rocket-like Yasir Arafat delivery out of the ground with only two balls remaining.

For a player who thrives on the adrenaline and excitement of T20, Zampa's off-field pursuits seem somewhat . . . sedate. The 24-year-old is happy to bide his time scouring second-hand shops in trendy inner-city suburbs for vintage relics, ranging from vinyl LPs by 1970s bands Foreigner or ELO to old corduroy hats. 'I'm amazed by what people throw away,' said the leg spinner. 'You always find little treasures. In Adelaide there's a place called Hindmarsh Disposals, which sells old furniture, and I have a little man cave at home with a pool table, a bar and old furniture, and that's where my old record player sits. I found some old records, and when I was a kid my dad played that stuff and I thought it was rubbish, but I appreciate it now.'

Getty Images

While Zampa proved his toughness by not even wincing when Dwayne Bravo smashed the ball back at the bridge of his nose and it crashed off onto the stumps, his big six off Arafat suggested he is a more than capable batsman. 'I think that opened a few doors,' he said. 'I had a couple of decent digs in one-day cricket batting at nine or 10, and I got a bit of confidence out of my batting from that and ended up batting at No. 6 [for South Australia] in the Sheffield Shield.'

Zampa, who was picked for Australia's one-day and T20 teams after BBL|05, said he decided to become a leg spinner the day he realised the odds were stacked against him as a fast bowler. 'I was a 14-year-old bowling medium pace and I tried to open the batting,' he said. 'I realised I wasn't going to be big enough or quick enough, and there were a lot of batters around, so I decided to do something different, went to the nets, started bowling leggies and they came out okay.'

MELBOURNE STARS

BBL|05

BOWLING

MATCHES:	10
OVERS:	38
MAIDENS:	0
WICKETS:	12
RUNS:	270
BBI:	2–16
AV:	22.50
ECON:	7.10
S/R:	19

FACT ATTACK

- As a teenager, Zampa played for Sutherland in Sydney's grade competition alongside Nic Maddinson and Steve Smith.
- His 6–19 for the Pune Supergiants in the 2016 Indian Premier League was the second best performance by an Indian Premier League bowler.
- He took an impressive 3–23 on a subcontinental pitch in Australia's World T20 win over Bangladesh.

LUKE WRIGHT

MEET MR WRIGHT

BBL|05

BATTING

MATCHES:	10
INNINGS:	10
NOT OUTS:	2
RUNS:	280
HS:	109*
AV:	35
BALLS FACED:	216
S/R:	129.62
SIXES:	7
FOURS:	34

FACT ATTACK

- Many consider Wright a white-ball specialist, but in 2013 and 2015 he averaged more than 50 in English County Cricket.
- Wright's son, Joshua, wants him to hit more sixes to trigger the fireworks that celebrate a big hit in the BBL.
- His Stars teammate Kevin Pietersen lashed out at England's selectors when Wright was left out of their 2016 World T20 side.

Englishman Luke Wright interpreted his former teammate Matt Wade's struggle to remember the Melbourne Stars' second import for BBL|05 as the ultimate form of Aussie acceptance. After reeling off Kevin Pietersen's name, Wade (who had just joined the Renegades from the Stars), struggled to recall that Wright—who has played 100 limited-overs matches for England—was the Stars' other foreign player. 'He'd forgotten it was me, because I'd been here so long,' Wright told the media. 'It's amazing. Even the crowd have forgotten I'm English.'

Apart from playing in England's T20 Blast and the BBL, Wright can also be found churning out runs in New Zealand, India, Bangladesh and Dubai. He insists, however, that life as a cricket 'freelancer' isn't always the glamorous existence some might imagine. 'I don't think people realise, until you're an overseas player, the sort of pressures on you,' he said. 'You're being brought in as a hired gun, so to speak, and there's a lot of pressure on that.'

Regardless, he's become an integral part of the Stars since signing for the inaugural 2011–12 BBL tournament. He was originally used at No. 6 or 7, but was promoted to opener when the Stars struggled to get good starts. The 31-year-old needed only his second appearance there to shine, hammering 117 off 60 balls against Hobart.

Wade wouldn't have needed any reminding that Wright was an import the night he tormented the Renegades with his masterful 109 not out in front of the record 80,883 crowd at the MCG. With five balls remaining, Wright secured a 7-wicket victory with his 11th four, adding lustre to his effort by smashing four sixes during his 66-ball innings.

Getty Images

'It's just unbelievable,' said Wright, moments after the adrenaline-charged innings in front of an appreciative crowd. 'You look around and you pinch yourself. 'We had a feeling it was going to be big tonight, but obviously not that big—and [in] a derby . . . it's probably one of the best cricketing moments I've had in my life.'

Apart from Wade's forgetfulness, another sign that Wright is an important part of the Stars' culture came two years ago when the club's chief executive Clint Cooper signed him to a long-term deal. 'You look at what he's done on the field and he's been a great signing,' Cooper told the press. 'But beyond that, if you consider the type of guy he is, he's just been a fabulous influence.'

DANIEL WORRALL

ARC ANGLE PUTS WORRALL ON COURSE

An obstacle in the in the middle of Daniel Worrall's childhood backyard played a significant role in shaping what's been described as one of the most unusual run-ups ever seen in the BBL.

Worrall, whose brilliant 3–15 against the Scorchers in Perth helped to secure the Stars a home semi final last summer, says his arc-like run-up is the legacy of needing to contend with a natural hazard when he played imaginary Test matches against his brothers.

Getty Images

'It all starts in the backyard,' laughed Worrall. 'We had two shocking trees and the only way you could bowl from a long run-up was to go around—it was as simple as that. I didn't play cricket until I was 15 or 16 and I didn't see any need to change it.'

The run-up has served Worrall well. Apart from finishing second on the Sheffield Shield's highest wicket-takers after taking 44 scalps for South Australia in 2015–16, he showed more than enough during his four games for the Stars to suggest he's also a bowler with a future in T20 cricket.

His 3–15 against the Scorchers excited plenty of experts, including his skipper David Hussey who described the effort as 'world-class'. It also pushed the 25-year-old to work hard during the winter to build on the inroads he made during BBL|05.

'It was important for me to fit in at that level last summer and after having had some reasonable success it's all about working hard,' he said. 'I'm working so I won't be a back-up bowler . . . I want to break into the starting XI and make an impact. 'Whether or not that happens remains to be seen, but I'm working hard to do it.'

As a cricketer who is stunned by how far he's come since playing in his first competition game with some mates 10 years ago, Worrall says he finds it 'surreal' to think players who he once considered to be 'heroes' are now his teammates at the Stars.

'I said throughout the BBL|05 that I had to pinch myself to make sure I wasn't dreaming and I meant it because I'm playing alongside guys who were my heroes a few years ago. It's incredible and while it is crazy to think I'll have a coffee with, say, Kevin Pietersen after training I've found that from playing alongside them I'm actually striving to be as good as them.'

MELBOURNE STARS

BBL|04

BOWLING

MATCHES:	4
OVERS:	15.3
MAIDENS:	0
WICKETS:	7
RUNS:	126
BBI:	3–15
AV:	18
ECON:	8.12
S/R:	13.2

FACT ATTACK

- He's nicknamed 'Frank' after his namesake, the great West Indian cricketer, who captained the West Indies.
- Worrall played the role of former World Series cricketer Mick Malone in the television series *Howzat*.
- Former South Australian coach Darren Berry lured him from Victoria because he liked Worrall's competitive streak.

RIGHT-HAND BATSMAN/RIGHT-ARM FAST-MEDIUM BOWLER

JOHN HASTINGS

TRUE GRIT

BBL|05

BATTING

MATCHES:	5
INNINGS:	1
NOT OUTS:	1
RUNS:	15
HS:	15*
AV:	–
BALLS FACED:	8
S/R:	187.50
SIXES:	1
FOURS:	1

BOWLING

MATCHES:	5
OVERS:	20
MAIDENS:	0
WICKETS:	8
RUNS:	170
BBI:	4-29
AV:	21.25
ECON:	8.50
S/R:	15.0

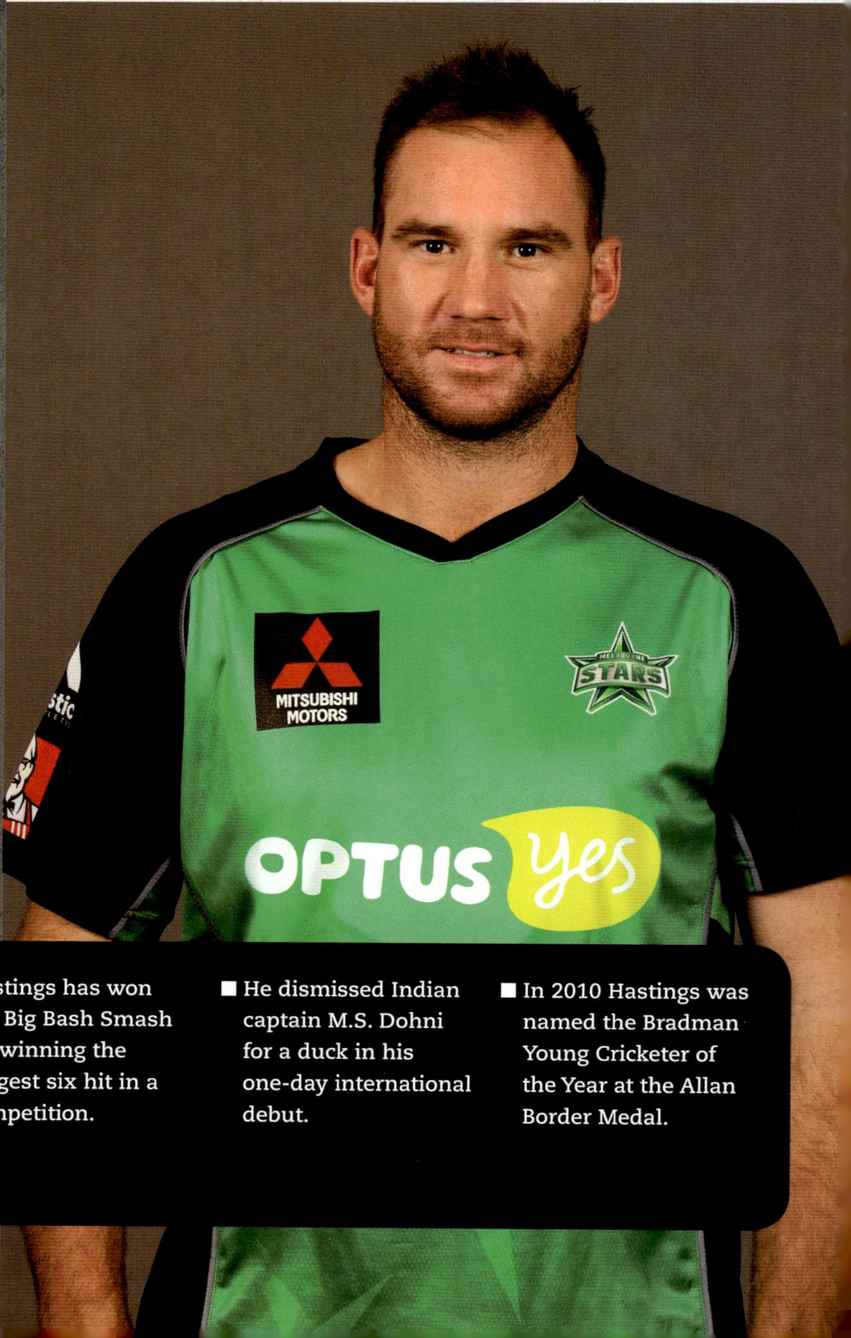

FACT ATTACK

- Hastings has won the Big Bash Smash for winning the longest six hit in a competition.
- He dismissed Indian captain M.S. Dohni for a duck in his one-day international debut.
- In 2010 Hastings was named the Bradman Young Cricketer of the Year at the Allan Border Medal.

He's nicknamed 'The Duke' because, like the legendary Hollywood actor, John Hastings's first two names are John Wayne, but the hulking Melbourne Stars all-rounder's determination to play with all guns blazing isn't an act.

While Hastings, who has represented Australia in each of the game's three formats, plays cricket because of the enjoyment it provides, he draws upon the unknown to give everything he possibly can for the Stars, Victoria or Australia.

'You don't know when you're going to play your last game,' he said. 'I know that sounds like a cliché but I think of Jarryd Roughhead [the AFL star]—and he's a ripping bloke—but he was unfortunately diagnosed with melanoma. To me it was a reminder that you can't tell the future so you have to go out and enjoy playing . . . you need to go out and make the most of every chance you get.'

Hastings, who came through the junior ranks with fellow internationals Stephen O'Keefe and Peter Forrest, said something he's always loved about cricket is the fact it's a test of character.

'Cricket isn't always what's written in the media,' he said. 'Sometimes you can go out to bat and get a first ball duck and the truth is there's nothing you can do about it because it was a beautiful ball.

'There's also those days when you can bowl a perfect yorker and it's squeezed behind point for four . . . so, yes, I do believe cricket is a true test of character, especially in T20 because there's so little margin for error and you're under so much scrutiny with the crowds at the grounds and television audiences watching at home.

'Sometimes in the BBL you can bowl really well but get whacked around the ground. It's tough, but what I've learnt is you have to stay strong and trust the processes.'

Getty Images

The powerfully-built Hastings explained his decision to turn his back on a promising rugby union career in Sydney for cricket was justified the day when he received his second rookie state contract.

'The second rookie deal made it count because I thought anyone can get one contract,' he said. 'However, to get a second one made me think that I had a future in the sport.'

And the good news for the Melbourne Stars' plan to be a heavyweight force is the motivation that pushes him means Hastings will go for broke every time he takes the field in BBL|06.

JOEL PARIS

FATHER, SON AND BOWLER'S SPIRIT

When Joel Paris was young, his father Mark, an all-rounder who captained Perth's Nedlands A-grade team in the 1980s, offered some advice that would help him to star one day for the Scorchers and represent Australia in limited-overs cricket. 'When he was seven I told him don't bother how many times you get driven through mid-off or through the covers, because if you don't pitch the ball up it will never swing,' said Mark. 'I explained captains can't set fields for short-pitched bowling, unless of course you're trying deliberately to get somebody out hooking, but at under-age cricket you want to be pitching the ball up to give it a chance to swing, and now he swings the ball pretty well.'

Getty Images

Paris, who wore Glenn McGrath's old No.11 when he made his one-day international debut against India at the WACA last summer, described his father as someone who never forgot that children's sport was about fun, making friends and forging character. 'It was always the drive home from a game where we spoke about footy or cricket—we'd get [the post-match review] out of the way,' said Paris. 'As soon as we got home and walked through the front door we'd leave it outside and move on.

'The discussions were sometimes harsh, but they were also always awfully fair, and Dad is one of the reasons why I've been able to do so well so far. When I was younger his approach was to have fun and enjoy it, but at the same time I made sure I listened to every little thing he tried to help me with.' Paris said he has built his career on his father's tip to pitch the ball up. 'That stuck with me,' he said. 'It's actually become my biggest weapon.'

Paris's proud father said his son's attitude was also an important cornerstone to his achievements, which include taking 6 wickets in his long-awaited Sheffield Shield debut for Western Australia against Victoria in 2015. 'He's also managed to deal with a lot of things in life that haven't gone his way—his injuries have been well documented over the past four or five years—but he's remained positive and continued to work through those, and his personality has allowed him to do that,' he said.

PERTH SCORCHERS

BBL|05

BOWLING

MATCHES:	7
OVERS:	25.1
MAIDENS:	0
WICKETS:	5
RUNS:	209
BBI:	2–39
AV:	41.80
ECON:	8.30
S/R:	30.2

FACT ATTACK

- Paris represented Western Australia's under-19s when he was 16.
- He played alongside Cameron Bancroft, Gurinder Sandhu and Kurtis Patterson in Australia's under-19 team.
- He took an unofficial hat-trick when he dismissed South Australia's Jake Weatherald with the first ball of a Shield game after taking wickets with the final two balls against Queensland.

RIGHT-HAND BATSMAN/RIGHT-HAND BOWLER

MITCHELL MARSH

THE RESILIENT ONE

BBL|05

BATTING

MATCHES:	1
INNINGS:	1
NOT OUTS:	0
RUNS:	1
HS:	1
AV:	1
BALLS FACED:	2
S/R:	50
SIXES:	0
FOURS:	0

BOWLING

OVERS:	2
MAIDENS:	0
WICKETS:	0
RUNS:	16
BBI:	0–16
AV:	–
ECON:	8
S/R:	–

FACT ATTACK

- Mitchell Marsh made his debut for Western Australia's one-day team aged 17 after he made 208 against Fremantle, making him his state's youngest debutant in 70 years.
- He captained Australia to victory in the 2010 Under-19 World Cup staged in New Zealand.
- He represented Western Australia at the 2008 AFL National Under-18 Championships.

Mitchell Marsh was taught plenty about the value of resilience when he grew up as a virtual bowling machine for his older brother—and Scorchers teammate—Shaun in their backyard Test battles. The Marsh brothers lived on a sprawling property south of Perth, and during the cricket season the family's tennis court might as well have been the WACA as the brothers battled it out.

Mitchell Marsh, who in an interview for the Scorchers' media department described himself as a 'ratbag' of a kid, recalled bowling marathon-like spells that would have left the likes of cricket's renowned workhorses, including Glenn McGrath and Dennis Lillee, gasping for breath in the sweltering Perth heat.

'We used to play a fair bit of backyard cricket and I'd bowl until Shaun had enough of batting,' said Marsh of the one-sided contests. 'He'd hit the ball out of the tennis court and into the bush, and that was the end of the game. How I became a batsman I don't know, because I used to bowl two or three hours [at a time] in backyard cricket.'

While Marsh only played one match for the Scorchers during BBL|05, he has a huge fan in Alan Davidson, the left-arm legend who made his Test debut in 1953 and is ranked alongside Keith Miller, Garfield Sobers and Jacques Kallis as one of cricket's great all-rounders. The pair met in 2015, when Davidson, then aged 85, presented Marsh with his Western Suburbs (Sydney) cap because Cricket Australia wanted the Western Australian to prove he was fit enough to represent the national one-day team in a match against India at the SCG.

Davidson, who played a starring role in cricket's historic first tied Test against the West Indies at the Gabba in 1960–61, was

Getty Images

adamant that 25-year-old Marsh has it in him to be one of the BBL's pin-up players. 'He has the right physique, his father Geoff played for Australia, his brother is in the national team, so cricket is in his family's genes,' said Davidson. 'And what I really liked about Mitch is from chatting to him I could see he's eager to learn. It's obvious to me that he wants to be better than he is, and if anything I think Mitch needs to develop supreme confidence . . . because in my opinion he has the skills and talent to be something special.'

SHAUN MARSH

LIVING UP TO SUPER STANDARDS

As a player whose early teenage years were spent travelling the world with the Australian cricket team his father Geoff coached in the 1990s, Shaun Marsh learnt early on what's needed to make the cut. He took particular interest in watching how his childhood idols Justin Langer and Steve Waugh prepared themselves as internationals and now, as one of the Perth Scorchers' genuine superstars, he still pushes himself to follow their example. 'I always loved Steve Waugh growing up. Dad played alongside him and then he coached him,' said Marsh. 'He was someone who I looked up to. I idolised him.'

Getty Images

'It was the same with Justin Langer, a left-hander like me. I was lucky enough to play cricket with him, and as my coach at Western Australia and the Scorchers he's had a big influence on my career. What I've learnt is one of the most important traits is to work as hard as you can on your game. Once you reach a certain level, working hard helps get you to where you want to be, but whether it's skill work or training in the gym, you need the dedication to work on all facets of the game.'

Marsh has enjoyed some spectacular moments since fulfilling his dream to become a first-class cricketer, including scoring a polished Sheffield Shield century against a Test-strength New South Wales XI at 19; making 81 in his one-day international debut against the West Indies in 2008; and becoming one of only 17 Australians [at that stage] to have scored a century on their Test debut, with 141 against Sri Lanka.

The popular Western Australian laid the foundations for his spectacular T20 career in 2008, when he finished the inaugural Indian Premier League as the tournament's leading run-scorer, with 616 runs at 68.44. He's proven just as brutally effective in the BBL, becoming one of only six players to crash through the 1000-run barrier. His five games for the Scorchers in BBL|05 were phenomenal, and he finished the summer with an average of 72.66.

Marsh said it shouldn't be a secret why some of the game's greatest players are throwing themselves into the hurly-burly excitement of Australia's T20 competition. 'The BBL has the whole package,' he enthused. 'You play in front of a big crowd, the standard of cricket is high, it's one of the best T20 competitions in the world and players also get to showcase their skills to huge television audiences.'

PERTH SCORCHERS

BBL|05

BATTING	
MATCHES:	5
INNINGS:	5
NOT OUTS:	2
RUNS:	218
HS:	76*
AV:	72.66
BALLS FACED:	170
S/R:	128.23
SIXES:	10
FOURS:	18

FACT ATTACK

- When asked for his thoughts on his son's game, Geoff Marsh told reporters, 'He's got a few more shots than me.'
- Shaun Marsh hit Mark Waugh's off spin for two consecutive sixes in 2003 to rack up his maiden first-class century for Western Australia.
- His sister Melissa played for West Coast in the Women's National Basketball League.

LEFT-HAND BATSMAN/LEFT-ARM ORTHODOX SPIN BOWLER

ASHTON AGAR

ONWARDS AND UPWARDS

BBL|05

BATTING

MATCHES:	8
INNINGS:	6
NOT OUTS:	1
RUNS:	124
HS:	68
AV:	24.80
BALLS FACED:	97
S/R:	127.83
SIXES:	5
FOURS:	10

BOWLING

OVERS:	9
MAIDENS:	0
WICKETS:	3
RUNS:	69
BBI:	2–38
AV:	23
ECON:	7.66
S/R:	18

FACT ATTACK

- While Agar says he modelled his game on his brother William, his youngest brother Wes represented Australia in the under-19 side.
- His father John is a former first-grade cricketer; his mother Sonia was born in Sri Lanka.
- He finished at Melbourne's De La Salle College in 2011 among the school's top 5 per cent of scholars.

Ashton Agar needed only one Test match—his debut during the 2013 Ashes—to rewrite the record books, smashing a gutsy 98 after being sent in as Australia's No. 11 batsman with his team on the ropes at 9–117. Aged 19, Agar displayed immense maturity, and grit, to join Phillip Hughes and take the fight to England. By the time his sensational 101-ball knock came to an end, when he was caught by Graeme Swann off Stuart Broad's bowling, he'd hit the highest individual score by a No. 11 Test batter; scored the second-fastest half-century by a No. 11 batter on debut; set a world record for the 10th-wicket partnership by scoring 163 with Hughes; surpassed Glenn McGrath's 61 as the highest score by an Aussie No. 11; and helped steer Australia to an unlikely 65-run lead over England.

While England's Joe Root and James Anderson broke the 10th-wicket record against India the following year, Agar is keen to move on from something he describes as a treasured memory. 'I'm reminded about it all the time,' he laughed. 'It's a memory that's a source of great pride and happiness, but it isn't a moment I'd like for my career to be defined by. It's something I want to keep building on and improving on. What I'd like when my career comes to an end—and I hope that isn't for another 15 years—is to be remembered as an accomplished all-rounder. I want the records to show I was someone who contributed with the bat, the ball and in the field.'

The 23-year-old is doing exactly that for the Scorchers, saying the excitement of the BBL draws out his best. 'I love the BBL because I get to express myself with the bat, the ball and out in the field,' he said. 'The nature of T20 cricket brings all-rounders into the game because you're a valuable member of your side when you contribute to each of the game's three aspects—batting, bowling and fielding.'

Getty Images

While Agar's versatility has made him a fan favourite at #TheFurnace, he's adamant BBL teams can't afford to be dominated by all-rounders. 'It's helpful being an all-rounder, but there are people with specific skill sets who perform really well in T20 games,' he said. 'There are guys who are huge hitters of the ball, guys who are fast bowlers but have an expertise in bowling yorkers; people have standout skills that put them at an advantage in T20 cricket.'

LEFT-ARM FAST-MEDIUM BOWLER

DOUG BOLLINGER

THE VETERAN

Sydney Sixers rookie Mickey Edwards, a 20-year-old express pace bowler with aspirations to become a paramedic, needed no time to nominate Doug Bollinger as the man who helped him find his feet in the BBL team's squad.

Bollinger is regarded as one of cricket's great characters, a player who mistakenly kissed a beer sponsor's logo rather than the national coat of arms when he took a Test wicket in New Zealand; who was such a pest the NSW team once bought him an iPod in the hope it would keep him quiet; a teammate who drove his peers in the Australian dressing room to despair with the same joke every day: Two fish are in a tank. One of them says, 'How do you drive this thing?'

When asked about the impact Bollinger has had on his burgeoning career, Edwards spoke instead of a seasoned professional with a willingness to share his hard-earned lessons. 'He's a great mentor and we young fast bowlers are quick to ask him for tips and advice, because Doug has been around the traps,' he enthused.

Bollinger, 35, has simple advice about life as a paceman, including how to deal with such things as the pressure of bowling at the death when a poor delivery can mean the difference between victory and defeat. 'There's always pressure and there's always nerves in a BBL game; it doesn't matter if you're bowling first and you want to keep the runs down or if you're bowling the last over and the game is on the line,' he said.

He says the secret to a fast bowler surviving in a game designed for big sixes and rapid runs is to take a deep breath sometimes. 'You need to really enjoy it,' he said. 'You need to take the game as it is, because you're going to bowl good balls that are hit for six and you're going to bowl bad balls that'll take wickets. You just need to take everything in and not put too much pressure on yourself to get wickets. I've learnt to let the game come, because 20 overs is quite a lot of cricket when you're out there batting or bowling.

'People ask about being hit for six and whether it hurts your fast bowler's pride, but you learn it's the nature of the beast. While it can be upsetting, you need to take yourself away from it, dust yourself off and focus on the next delivery.'

Getty Images

BBL|05

BOWLING

MATCHES:	8
OVERS:	26.4
MAIDENS:	0
WICKETS:	7
RUNS:	219
BBI:	2–31
AV:	31.28
ECON:	8.21
S/R:	22.8

FACT ATTACK

- Three years before making his debut for the NSW Sheffield Shield team, Bollinger was a park cricketer for the Seven Hills Toongabbie RSL team.
- In 2010 he was named in the ICC's Test and one-day international teams of the year.
- Bollinger is a specialist fast-bowling coach at the Sydney Sixers Academy, and hopes to build on that role in the years to come.

RIGHT-HAND BATSMAN/RIGHT-ARM FAST-MEDIUM BOWLER

SEAN ABBOTT

THE FIGHTER

BBL|05

BATTING	
MATCHES:	8
INNINGS:	7
NOT OUTS:	2
RUNS:	25
HS:	7*
AV:	5
BALLS FACED:	34
S/R:	73.52

BOWLING	
OVERS:	21.3
MAIDENS:	0
WICKETS:	11
RUNS:	215
BBI:	3–8
AV:	19.54
ECON:	10
S/R:	11.7

FACT ATTACK

- Abbott represented the Parramatta Eels' under-16 rugby league team in 2008.
- He made his debut for the NSW one-day team when he was 18 years old.
- He was the 'youngest'-ever international, being picked to represent Australia after his fifth birthday. He was born in a leap year.

Sean Abbott couldn't have staged a better return from his nightmare at Adelaide Oval—when Strikers ramrod Travis Head smashed 45 runs off nine of his deliveries to win the game—than his inspiring effort against Brisbane. Sixers bowling coach Geoff Lawson described Abbott's final over of the SCG match against the Heat—in which the 23-year-old was at one stage on a hat-trick, unleashed a 142 km/h yorker, and even produced some spin—as among the best performances he'd seen. His 3–8 from two overs was the perfect comeback from a horrific New Year's Eve, when Head single-handedly led the Strikers to a stunning victory at Abbott's expense, hitting three consecutive sixes off his final over to finish the game.

Lawson, who has long described Abbott as a hard worker with a willingness to learn, described the fightback as the sign of a player with an indomitable spirit. 'Sean worked very hard to sort things out, and he worked on a few new deliveries—and he landed them perfectly,' recalled Lawson. 'It was a great sign for the future. He only worked on the [spin] for a few weeks; he didn't have the confidence to bowl it [before], but before the match we just said go for it, and he now has a mixture of deliveries.'

Abbott—who mentors the Parramatta under-16 representative junior cricket team for which he played eight years ago—advises youngsters there's one crucial criterion for succeeding in the T20 arena. 'You have to be adaptable,' he said. 'There are only 20 overs in an innings but there's so many situations you can find yourself in during a game. If someone isn't bowling well, you're going to have to step up and bowl at the end or at the top [of the innings] with a new ball and only two fielders [in the deep].

'The captain can throw you the ball at any stage or he could ask you to field in any particular position, so you always need to be ready. And, if the team is losing wickets, you need to be able to go out and bat for a few overs without, for lack of a better word, slogging. In T20 a player needs to be prepared to play in any position of a game because it can move so fast. You're never really out of it; it only takes one over to get back into a game.'

NATHAN LYON

SPIN-BALL WIZARD

Nathan Lyon credits the sloping pitch on which he and his brother played their backyard Tests, in the NSW Central West town of Young, with making him a strike weapon for the Sydney Sixers and Australia. He says that as a young boy, lacking the muscle needed to bowl up the slope encouraged him to embrace a bowling style that's allowed him to become Australia's most successful exponent of off spin.

'My brother Brendan bowled leg spin and I wanted to do something bigger and better than him, so I bowled off spin—and it's paid off so far,' said Lyon, recalling the origins of his brilliant career. 'Ours was a small backyard with a slope. Brendan always bowled the ball so it spun down the hill. I was never strong enough to spin it up the hill, so I had to go off spin so I could turn it back down the slope to him.'

Lyon's Sixers teammates, including Brad Haddin and Steve O'Keefe, talk openly about his resilience, the trait that's allowed him to nail down his role as Australia's Test spin bowler after the selectors trialled 12 men for the job in the four years after Shane Warne's retirement in 2007.

Haddin was behind the stumps when Lyon bowled what some have described as the greatest-ever opening over in BBL history. The spinner took the wickets of Hobart superstars Tim Paine and Kumar Sangakkara in their BBL|05 clash at the SCG to set up an inspiring victory. 'He's always challenging himself and asks a lot of questions,' Haddin said. 'He leads by his actions and his will to improve when he turns up to training.'

Lyon said if young cricketers could take anything from his success it would be the value of wanting to learn. 'I'm a big one for training hard and having a good work ethic,' he said. 'If that can provide an example for the younger guys who'll be coming into the squad, then I'm all for that. I watched to see what guys did at training [for New South Wales and Australia] and how they got better. I never compared myself to those guys in the athletic stakes, but I kept a keen eye on what it was they did to improve their skills, and I learnt a lot about mental preparation and match preparation.'

BBL|05

BOWLING

MATCHES:	4
OVERS:	15.5
MAIDENS:	0
WICKETS:	7
RUNS:	111
BBI:	5–23
AV:	15.85
ECON:	7.01
S/R:	13.5

FACT ATTACK

- When Lyon took the most wickets by an Australian off spinner he was nicknamed GOAT—greatest of all time—by his teammates.
- He was working as a member of the Adelaide ground staff when he was selected to play for South Australia's T20 team.
- Lyon dismissed Sri Lanka's Kumar Sangakkara with the first ball he bowled in Test cricket.

MITCHELL STARC

AN OUTSTANDING PARTNERSHIP

BBL|01 to BBL|04

BOWLING

MATCHES:	10
OVERS:	37.3
MAIDENS:	0
WICKETS:	20
RUNS:	297
BBI:	3–17
AV:	14.85
ECON:	7.92
S/R:	11.2

FACT ATTACK

- Starc was named the 2015 ICC World Cup's best player after taking 22 wickets at an average of 10.18.
- His brother Brandon was selected to represent Australia in high jump at the Rio de Janeiro Olympics.
- Starc and Alyssa Healy join England's Roger and Ruth Prideaux and Sri Lanka's Guy de Alwis and Rasanjali Silva as married couples who have played Test cricket.

Mitchell Starc and his wife Alyssa Healy (see inset photo) are poised to create a unique slice of history during BBL|06, by becoming the first husband-and-wife team to represent the Sydney Sixers (or indeed any BBL franchise).

Injury and his commitments to the national team prevented Starc—who was named the best player of the 2015 ICC World Cup tournament—from taking the new ball in a tough BBL|05 campaign for the Sixers. He used his stint on the sideline to support Healy and the Sixers' WBBL team as they rebounded from starting their season with six straight losses to qualify for the final. The left-arm fast bowler and the Wallabies rugby star Matt Toomua, who married Ellyse Perry on the weekend she hit the winning runs against the Perth Scorchers at the SCG, formed the male equivalent of the WAGs: the HABs—husbands and boyfriends.

'While it was unfortunate to see them get beaten in the final it's great that we have that "talk" between the two [Sixers] teams,' said Starc. 'They've been to a final, we've won one, and while [the men's team] didn't have a great tournament last summer, it's great to have that cross-team experience. I'm looking forward to the day when Alyssa and I play for the Sixers on the same day, because it'll be special.'

Starc says he has a good reason to feel proud of his place in the Sixers. 'I love that I was here for the first year and that there's a core group of players from BBL|01 still here,' he said. 'That was a huge year for us, winning the BBL title and the Champion's League, and we take a lot of pride in those titles. That was our benchmark season. It's where we want to get to every year. We take pride in our record at the club . . . and in our [dominant win–loss] record over [cross-town rivals] the Thunder.'

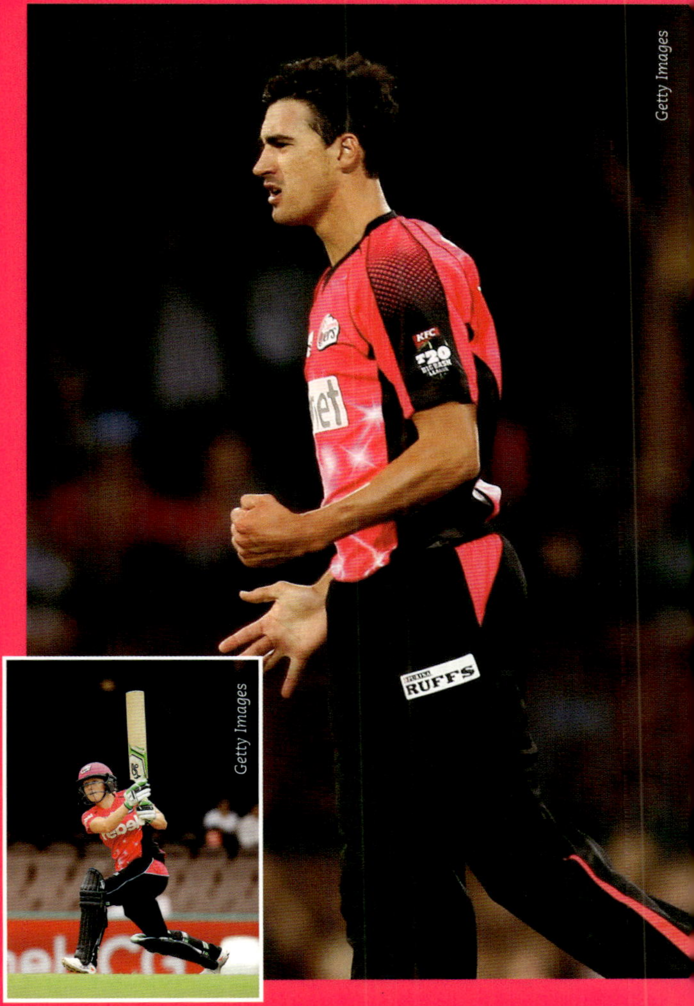

Getty Images

Getty Images

Starc said if his 2016–17 schedule allows him to galvanise the Sixers' BBL|06 attack, he'll go full throttle. 'It's not like a Test match, where you try to conserve your energy. It's four overs—that's 24 balls—and you bowl them as fast as you can,' he said. 'Execution is the key. I try to swing the new ball, and because I'm generally used for the last two overs, I hope there's a bit of reverse swing, and I try to hit those stumps when I bowl my yorkers.'

BEN ROHRER

BIG BEN STRIKES A WINNING BLOW

While Ben Rohrer hasn't watched the entire DVD of his team's memorable triumph to beat the Melbourne Stars for the BBL|05 champion's title, the 35-year-old admits he's almost worn out the vision of his almighty six that sealed the victory.

'I must admit I have watched that last ball a few times . . . quite a few times,' he said with a laugh. 'It's great because even though you can never be in that moment again watching it at least allows for me to relive the excitement I felt. It always provides a little bit of a thrill because it takes you back to where you were . . . a reminder of how exciting the night was. Whenever I watch that vision it gives me a bit of a pep up.'

Rohrer's impact on the Thunder throughout 2015–16 was far greater than his widely celebrated big hit at the MCG because in a season where the Thunder's big four—Mike Hussey, Jacques Kallis, Shane Watson and Andre Russell—received plenty of attention, the Australian T20 international was an unsung hero.

Getty Images

Apart from finishing the summer with an impressive strike rate of 138.15 after slamming 105 runs from the 76 deliveries he faced, Rohrer proved to be especially dangerous in the field with three of his laser-like throws from the deep running out batters.

Rohrer added to the Thunder's enviable depth of experience when he was targeted to return to Sydney after a successful stint with the Melbourne Renegades. He's adamant the accumulation of a core of wise old heads to complement the Thunder's brigade of fearless young guns played an important role in the team's ultimate success.

'When [coach] Paddy Upton and Mike Hussey linked up a few years ago they planned to assemble a good group of not so much the most talented players, but a group of good people who'd gel,' he said.

'They strived towards getting that and what I liked was the understanding among the players. From day one the feeling was we were there to work towards one common goal and we embraced the idea that the Thunder isn't about the individual . . . our team comes first.

'Now "Huss" has retired it's going to be crucial that a few of us older blokes step up and help our captain try to replace the irreplaceable qualities that Mike Hussey offered us.'

BBL|05

BATTING

MATCHES:	10
INNINGS:	8
NOT OUTS:	4
RUNS:	105
HS:	30
AV:	26.25
BALLS FACED:	76
S/R:	138.15
SIXES:	3
FOURS:	8

FACT ATTACK

- In 2007 Rohrer became the first player since Rod Davison in 1993–94 to score a first-class century on debut for New South Wales.
- He attended East Hills Boys High in Sydney's south-west, the same education institution that produced the Waugh brothers and Olympic swimming champion Ian Thorpe.
- He was selected to represent Australia against the West Indies in a T20 international at the Gabba. Rohrer scored 16 before being dismissed by Kieron Pollard.

RIGHT-ARM FAST-MEDIUM BOWLER

CLINT McKAY

MIND OVER BATTER

BBL|05

BOWLING

MATCHES:	10
OVERS:	33.5
MAIDENS:	1
WICKETS:	18
RUNS:	274
BBI:	4–28
AV:	15.22
ECON:	8.09
S/R:	11.2

FACT ATTACK

- McKay was named Australia's one-day international cricketer of the year at the 2013 Allan Border Medal awards night.
- In 2015 he helped spearhead English county team Leicestershire to its first victory in 992 days (more than two years, eight and a half months).
- He captured the prized wickets of Sachin Tendulkar and M.S. Dhoni in his one-day international debut against India in 2009.

During a BBL season when commentators questioned the legitimacy of the monster bats some players used to slay attacks, Clint McKay provided an insight into the attitude that allowed him to finish as the tournament's leading wicket-taker, insisting that the onus is on the bowlers to outwit technology.

Many bowlers were frustrated to see sixes scored off their bowling when the ball was snicked off the edge of the big bats, but the 33-year-old from Victoria described getting caught up in the debate as a waste of energy. 'If the bat companies can produce those bats within the rules and regulations, then good luck to them,' said McKay, who captured 18 wickets for the title-winning Thunder. 'You see other sports developing their technology—there's guys in golf hitting the ball so much further than they did 10 years ago—so we just need to get smarter as bowlers. It's not about having to counter technology—a good ball is a good ball, and if you execute your skill perfectly each time you're going to succeed as a bowler. The bowlers have to become better than the batter and stay one step ahead of the game.'

While he isn't blessed with express pace, McKay kept one step ahead in a brand of cricket that's about overcoming pressure by utilising his unerring accuracy, a hint of seam movement and a lethal back-of-the-hand slower ball that confounded the best players. 'When you're in the game for a long time, you learn what you dished up the ball before can't be changed,' he said.

'I was one of those guys at the start of my career who'd worry about the previous ball, but in time I realised the most important ball is the next one. It's important to stay relaxed so you can think clearly under pressure. It isn't easy. As soon as you walk out in front of a crowd of 48,000 people it's a massive pressure cooker. You just need to realise that all you have to do, and it's the one thing you can control, is run in and bowl.'

McKay remained modest about his feats throughout BBL|05 by attributing some of his wickets to luck. 'You don't look at personal milestones,' he said. 'But when [my finishing as the tournament's leading wicket-taker] is brought up, I feel quite happy and proud, because at the end of the day if I'm taking wickets I'm helping the Thunder achieve our aims.'

USMAN KHAWAJA

THE LOYAL SOLDIER

Usman Khawaja, still sweating after guiding the Thunder to a fairytale final berth on the back of his unbeaten 104 against the Strikers at Adelaide Oval, took time out from the celebrations to reveal how he was scarred by the franchise's four previous bleak years.

Before BBL|05, the Thunder was derided to by the likes of Sydney Sixers star bowler Mitchell Starc as 'The Chunder' because of the team's poor record. Khawaja, a foundation member, admitted it took a heart to heart with skipper Michael Hussey for him to remain in the electric green playing colours. 'It was tough because you play cricket to win and you're not winning and you're trying your best and still not winning; you're trying your best again and you're still not winning. It's a bit of a helpless feeling at times,' Khawaja said of the Thunder's five wins from 31 matches in the four seasons before taking out the crown. 'There were times when I thought, "Do I want to be in this team still? What do I want to do?" But when Huss came on board I thought we had a really good chance of picking this team up.'

Getty Images

When it came to the crunch, in the adrenaline-charged final against the Melbourne Stars, Khawaja played yet another winning hand. His 70 from 40 balls provided the foundation for the Thunder to mow down the 177 needed for victory.

While Hussey attributed Khawaja's form to his finding 'the zone', the 29-year-old explained that he'd excelled in BBL|05 because he learnt how to cope with the pressure—and heavy expectation. 'Growing up, I never played cricket well when I put too much pressure on myself or if I took the game too seriously,' he said. 'I just don't do it anymore. I go out there and have fun. Even before I bat I'm jumping around, I'm not really serious, going out there like it's any other day, any other game. That's the only way I can enjoy my cricket.'

While national selector Mark Waugh declared during the final that Khawaja was batting better than Windies great Brian Lara, the man known as Usie offered young cricketers great advice in deflecting attention from himself after being named man of the Big Final. 'I don't play here for individual success,' he said. 'Nothing feels as good as winning a championship. No matter how many hundreds you score, or how many man of the matches you get, nothing compares to winning something with your teammates.'

SYDNEY THUNDER

BBL|05

BATTING

MATCHES:	4
INNINGS:	4
NOT OUTS:	2
RUNS:	345
HS:	109*
AV:	172.50
BALLS FACED:	211
S/R:	163.50
CENTURIES:	2
HALF-CENTURIES:	2
SIXES:	10
FOURS:	39

FACT ATTACK

- Khawaja was born in Islamabad, Pakistan, and moved to Sydney with his family when he was a young boy.
- He obtained his pilot's licence before his driver's licence.
- He was selected to make his Test debut in 2011, as the replacement for injured Australian skipper Ricky Ponting.

RIGHT-HAND BATSMAN/RIGHT-ARM FAST-MEDIUM BOWLER

SHANE WATSON

THE MENTOR

BBL|05

BATTING

MATCHES:	10
INNINGS:	10
NOT OUTS:	0
RUNS:	235
HS:	66
AV:	23.50
BALLS FACED:	178
S/R:	132.02
SIXES:	13
FOURS:	17

BOWLING

OVERS:	28.2
MAIDENS:	0
WICKETS:	9
RUNS:	231
BBI:	3–13
AV:	25.66
ECON:	8.15
S/R:	18.8

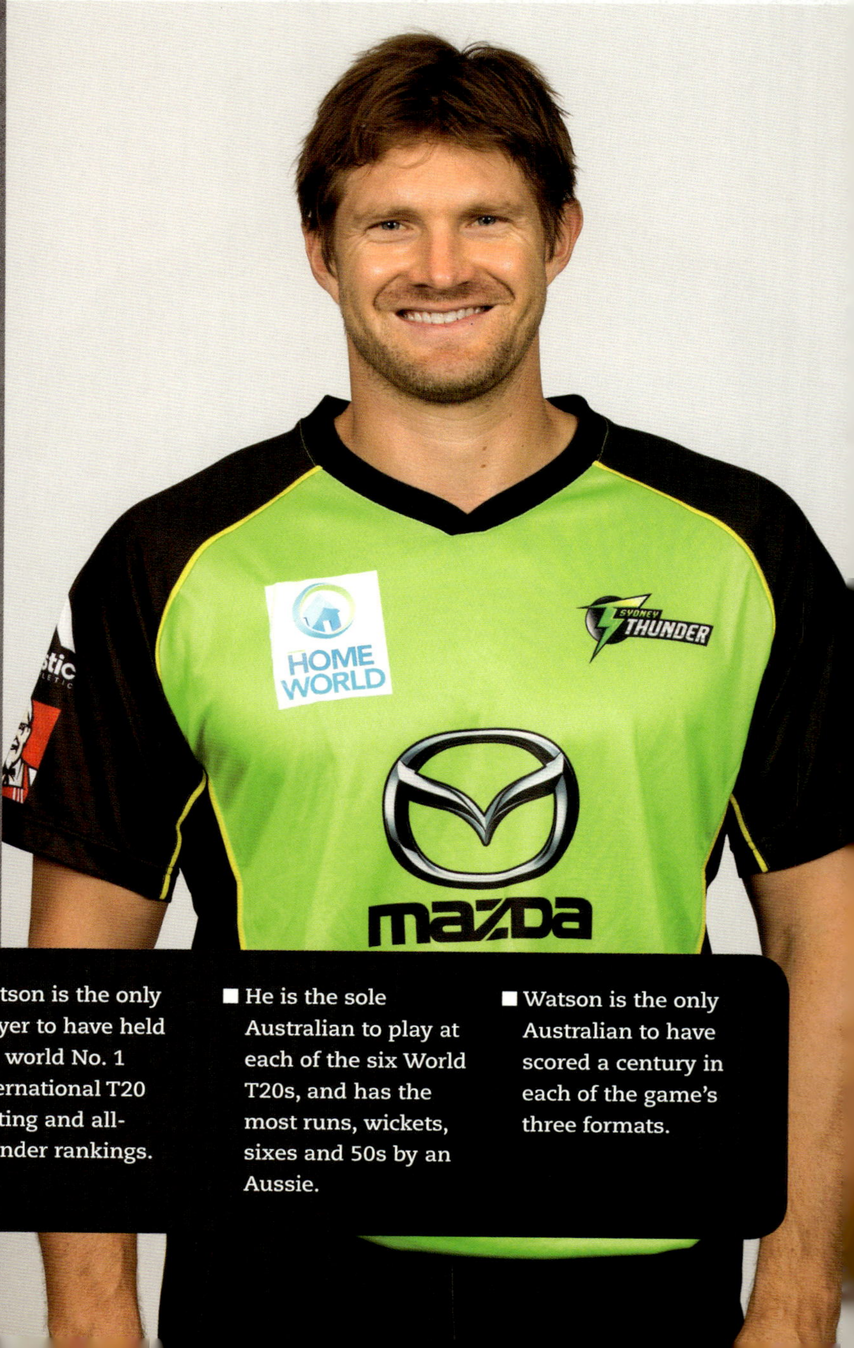

FACT ATTACK

- Watson is the only player to have held the world No. 1 international T20 batting and all-rounder rankings.
- He is the sole Australian to play at each of the six World T20s, and has the most runs, wickets, sixes and 50s by an Aussie.
- Watson is the only Australian to have scored a century in each of the game's three formats.

After 11 years of torment and rallying against his army of critics—and the social media trolls who picked on everything from his footwork to injuries—Shane Watson 'let go of the rope' during BBL|05 after being dropped from the Australian Test and one-day international teams—and he flourished.

As the all-rounder's apparent demise as an international dominated the media, Watson, who'd played 59 Tests and 190 one-day internationals, backed up his declaration that the Thunder was his priority with runs, wickets and catches, and by supporting his skipper, Mike Hussey, with strong leadership.

While his critics penned their epitaphs for his international career, Watson expressed a sense of liberation. 'Getting dropped from both formats—Test and one-day cricket—makes that worry go away,' he said of any pressure he'd put on himself to play at the 2016 World T20 (although he was chosen thanks to his high volume of runs and wickets). 'I love playing with the Thunder. It's an exciting franchise; it's nice that they want me as well. I want to be here; that's all that matters. The worry is gone, and disappeared after I got dropped from the one-day squad. I still definitely feel I have a lot to offer when I'm at my best.'

Watson was signed to play for the Thunder in BBL|05 after the team's management identified him a natural successor for the retirement-bound Hussey. He revealed that he chose to play in the electric green because he could sense it was a franchise on the rise. 'There looked as though there'd been good improvement [in BBL|04], and Nick Cummins, the chief executive, is an incredibly impressive man—one of the best CEO's I've had anything to do with in and around cricket,' he said. 'The idea of being able to

Getty Images

contribute with my experience, and the chance to play with Mike Hussey [in BBL|05] but also Jacques Kallis—he was my hero throughout my career—made it an incredible opportunity.'

With his extensive experience—and after his battles to stay in the Aussie teams—Watson said it was his plan to have a positive influence on other players' careers long after he retires. 'After I finish playing I want to stay in cricket. It's a game I absolutely love, it's given me an incredible life, and I want to contribute back to it even when I finish playing as well. The more I learn about these great players I play alongside, the more I'll be able to help out later on.'

GOBSMACKING MOMENTS

HEAD OF THE CLASS

Travis Head walking on air after arguably the greatest innings in BBL history. He smashed 56 off the final 15 deliveries to allow Adelaide to steam home against the shellshocked Sixers.

Adelaide Strikers v Sydney Sixers
31 December 2015, Adelaide Oval

Travis Head kept his . . . head . . . and in the process broke the Sydney Sixers' collective heart by igniting the New Year's Eve fireworks prematurely at Adelaide Oval with a knock described as the BBL's best-ever innings.

With three overs remaining and a head-spinning 51 runs needed for victory, the home team appeared done and dusted when Head took strike—and he sizzled!

He smashed 27 runs off Sean Abbott's second last over; belted 11 runs off Doug Bollinger in the 19th; and with 13 runs required off the final six balls the left-hander ignored the crackling atmosphere to shape up for Abbott's final over. He clubbed each of Abbott's first three deliveries for consecutive sixes to seal an incredible victory and in doing so the 22-year-old became the first Striker to hit a BBL century.

As the 46,389-strong crowd saluted its hero, a battalion of statisticians were dumbstruck as they dissected a knock to remember. They noted Head hammered 56 off the final 15 deliveries he faced; he needed only 53 deliveries to score his century; his unconquered 101 included nine sixes—seven of which came from his last 14 balls—and his milestone century was brought up with a towering six.

However, moments after securing a great victory Head admitted to Network Ten there were moments when he feared the job was beyond him.

ZAMPA WINS BY A NOSE

Melbourne Stars v Melbourne Renegades
Etihad Stadium, 9 January 2016

Forget Shane Warne's mystery 'zooter' ball, Melbourne Stars leg spin bowler Adam Zampa used his 'hooter' to dismiss Renegades batsman Peter Nevill in perhaps the BBL's most bizarre dismissal.

Zampa's nose took the full brunt of a ball smashed down the wicket by power-hitting West Indian import Dwayne Bravo. The ball ricocheted off non-striker Nevill's bat before cannonballing into the leg spinner's face when he dived to field it. The ball deflected from the bridge of Zampa's nose and crashed into the stumps, dislodging the bails.

Rather than reel away in agony, Zampa appealed to the umpire for a run-out. 'As soon as it hit the stumps I said howzat,' Zampa told reporters after the match. 'I realised what had happened. I've actually got to say sorry to [Nevill], because he was trying to be quite sympathetic and I just brushed him off and said, "That's out." '

Nevill himself said he was concerned for his opponent and had no idea that he was out: 'I didn't realise. [Umpire] Geoff Joshua had to tap me on the shoulder and say, "By the way, mate, you're out." My primary concern was Zamps. As soon as I'd seen what happened—and the sound that it made was pretty sickening—my primary concern was how he was doing.'

While his teammates described the sound of the six-stitcher crunching into Zampa's nose as disgusting, the man himself celebrated the Stars' 8-wicket victory by laughing off the league's most unusual dismissal, suggesting, 'It's a direct hit, isn't it?'

'The Hooter' Melbourne Stars spin bowler Adam Zampa attempts to stop the bleeding after the ball rebounded off his nose to run out Renegades batter Peter Nevill.

Dan Christian unleashes hell at the Gabba, launching a Luke Feldman delivery 117 metres onto the grandstand roof. A drone couldn't even locate it the following day.

CHRISTIAN ROARS IN THE LIONS' DEN

Brisbane Heat v Hobart Hurricanes
The Gabba, 29 December 2015

'I swung as hard as I could and it landed exactly where I wanted it to. It came out of the middle of the bat . . .' With that, Hobart Hurricanes all-rounder Dan Christian recalled how he hit what's hailed as the biggest six struck at the Gabba in living memory, launching a Luke Feldman delivery 117 metres away onto the grandstand's roof. Adding lustre to the legend of the big hit was the revelation that Christian's trusty blade was broken before he sent the ball rocketing into orbit.

Christian savaged 25 runs off Feldman in the second-last over, but no shot pleased him quite like the beauty that went viral on social media seconds after it the ball left his blade. 'I was waiting for it to come down in front of the sails but it kept going,' said Christian, who scored 56 runs off 24 deliveries. 'That's when I realised it was a decent one.'

Days after Christian's massive shot, a drone company part-owned by former Queensland Bulls batsman Lee Carseldine sent one of its contraptions on a sortie to locate the ball. The mission was abandoned, however, when the operator realised that the vast amount of metal in the grandstand, and the nearby mobile-phone towers, could interfere with his signals to the drone. The craft filmed some of the roof before the drone's operators cancelled the search, meaning the ball Christian slammed into orbit remains missing in action.

LYNN-SANITY AT THE MCG

Five sixes from five balls at the MCG, Brisbane Heat's master batter Chris Lynn proved why he was BBL|05's most destructive batsman.

Brisbane Heat v Melbourne Stars
MCG, 14 January 2016

When Chris Lynn bludgeoned five consecutive sixes off former Test bowler Ben Hilfenhaus, he not only navigated the bottom-placed Brisbane Heat to a stunning 56-run thrashing of the Melbourne Stars but he also made his candidacy for selection in Australia's World T20 impossible to ignore.

Lynn punished Hilfenhaus during the powerplay to rocket to his half-century off only 19 deliveries, and the MCG crowd was stunned as ball after ball soared deep into the stands. Try as he might, Hilfenhaus couldn't stem the flow of big hits. Lynn credited the strong breeze—it must've had cyclonic force—with each of his sixes landing an average 93 metres away. 'There are players around the world bowlers do get a bit twitchy about, so hopefully if I keep doing that I might be one of those,' he told reporters after falling to Adam Zampa on 56.

Lynn also provided an insight into the cavalier spirit that allowed for him to score 27 sixes among his season's tally of 378 runs. He conceded that he realised most batsmen would probably have opted to play it safe after clearing the boundary for a second consecutive time. 'If you can do it once, why don't you just keep your shape and go through the same process again and again?' he asked reporters.

KHAWAJA HAS THE POWER

Sydney Thunder v Melbourne Stars
MCG, 20 December 2015

After being sidelined for five weeks with a hamstring injury, Usman Khawaja needed only 70 balls to score an unconquered 109; dismiss the perception he isn't suited to limited-overs cricket; showcase his power game; and prove to the national selectors he was ready to return to the Test team for the Boxing Day Test.

The Sydney Thunder star, who tore his hamstring in a Test against New Zealand, later admitted that he needed to block the voice of treason from his mind when he fielded against the Stars. 'When I went out to field I was a little bit anxious, but the longer I was out there the better I felt,' he said after Sydney's stunning 1-run victory. 'I just kept saying, "You've done the work, if it happens now, so be it." There's not much more I can do, I've done everything I can.'

Khawaja's hamstring stood up to the test as he slaughtered the Stars' attack with a combination of elegant strokes and brutal blows to hit 12 boundaries and three sixes. After the match, the stunned Stars skipper, David Hussey, conceded that he'd never considered the 29-year-old to be a force in the T20 game.

'That's the one thing I've been working on in the last two or three years,' Khawaja said. 'It's come into my one-day game a little bit.

Usman Khawaja silenced those critics who thought his game wasn't suited for the short-form format by hammering an unconquered 109 which included 12 boundaries and three sixes.

It's just something that hasn't been natural to me. You see Andre Russell come in and hit sixes 50 rows back, and that's never going to be me. I've figured out other ways to score, figured out ways to get better at power hitting.'

Getty Images

Luke Wright nailed a brilliant century but the 80,883-strong crowd were enthralled by a 10-year-old boy who ate a watermelon bigger than his own head throughout the knock.

#WATERMELON BOY'S APPETITE FOR FAME

Melbourne Stars v Melbourne Renegades
MCG, 2 January 2016

Melbourne Stars opener Luke Wright scored an unconquered 109 off 63 balls in the cross-town derby against the Renegades, and while a record 80,883 spectators roared their approval, a 10-year-old boy who munched his way through a watermelon bigger than his own head stole the English import's thunder.

The action away from the action at a BBL match can be just as exciting as a towering six or a set of stumps being destroyed by a fireball. Over the years, classic catches taken by fans in the stands or the angry seagull that was revived after being splattered by a ball in the outfield during BBL|04 have sent social media into overdrive.

In BBL|05, however, the accidental star was Melbourne schoolboy Mitchell Schibeci, who wanted to become famous by appearing on the MCG's gigantic screen for doing something out of the ordinary. Not long after Mitchell settled into his seat for the WBBL preliminary match, the commentators spotted him munching into the melon—skin and all—and his progress was monitored throughout the match.

Adults gathered around him to take selfies, and when he finally appeared on the big screen, the image of him biting a chunk of the rind was greeted with a wild cheer from the mob. The Twittersphere and Facebook went into meltdown as #WatermelonBoy trended, and his effort was even covered by international news agencies.

Mitchell told Channel 9's *Today* program that he ate the watermelon to be noticed. 'I've seen people do weird stuff and they got on the big screen, so I thought I might do it myself,' he said, not sounding the least bit . . . seedy!

Ashton Agar is congratulated by his Perth Scorchers teammates after he flew like superman to dismiss Adelaide dangerman Brad Hodge at #TheFurnace.

AIRBORNE AGAR'S 'SPECCY' DISLODGES HODGE

Perth Scorchers v Adelaide Strikers #TheFurnace, 21 December 2015

Ashton Agar proved in his Test debut against England—when he came in at No. 11 to score 98 runs—that cometh the hour, he's a man equal to any challenge. One of Agar's greatest tests during BBL|05 came only two balls after he stepped onto #TheFurnace as a fielder to replace Nathan Coulter-Nile, who had dislocated his shoulder diving to field a ball.

The 22-year-old was welcomed to the action when the Strikers danger man, Brad Hodge, cracked a Joel Paris delivery when he was on 14 runs. Agar, fielding in the outfield, needed to run backwards to meet the flight of the rocketing ball, then dive to take a catch commentators immediately described as a contender for catch of the season.

Agar caught the ball with both hands, crashed into the ground with a thud, then tumble-turned as a result of his momentum, dislodging his sunglasses. Nevertheless, he somehow kept his grip on the ball and, although he stretched out his arms in triumph, no one seemed more amazed by his feat than the man himself.

This effort to dislodge Hodge wasn't the first time Agar had stunned Scorcher crowds with his athleticism—and courage. During BBL|04, Agar took an equally spectacular catch to dismiss the Sydney Sixers destroyer Nic Maddinson for only 2 runs, running towards the long-on fence to snaffle the chance over his shoulder.

Gayle-force: West Indies master blaster Chris Gayle needed only 12 balls to blast the world's equal fastest half-century when he took to Adelaide's attack.

GAYLE-FORCE DESTRUCTION

Melbourne Renegades v Adelaide Strikers
Etihad Stadium, 18 January 2016

Master blaster Chris Gayle made plenty of headlines off-field in BBL|05, but whenever the self-proclaimed 'Universe Boss' expressed himself through his batting, he was untouchable.

Gayle used his innings against the Adelaide Strikers—a match in which the Melbourne Renegades needed to score 171 in 16 overs to leapfrog the Thunder into the finals—to shine, hammering a 12-ball half-century that left even his harshest critics gasping. His innings included seven sixes, four of which were hit from consecutive deliveries bowled by Greg West. He was on 44 from 11 deliveries; in hitting a six from the next ball to bring up his 50, he equalled the world record set by India's Yuvraj Singh.

Adelaide coach Jason Gillespie watched on helplessly as the Gayle-force whirlwind blew his attack to pieces. 'We all know Chris Gayle is an amazing striker of the ball,' said Gillespie. 'When he's on, he's on.'

The Renegades stormed to 2–53 off only three overs, but Travis Head's gentle spin wreaked havoc in the fourth over when he dismissed Cameron White for 6, then removed Dwayne Bravo with his next delivery. Head, one of BBL|05's most destructive batsmen, sent Gayle packing in the sixth over. The West Indian's dismissal signalled the beginning of the end for the Renegades.

OLD BULL VERSUS YOUNG TURK

Sydney Thunder v Melbourne Stars
MCG, 20 December 2015

Melbourne Stars all-rounder James Faulkner went for broke in his tense final over duel with the Sydney Thunder's Jacques Kallis at the MCG.

When Melbourne Stars 25-year-old all-rounder James Faulkner took strike against 40-year-old South African great Jacques Kallis needing 10 runs from the final over to win the match, it was a continuation of the age-old duel between youth and experience.

Faulkner, considered one of T20's best finishers, appeared on track to bring his team home in front of an enthusiastic MCG crowd when he scored 6 of the required runs from Kallis's first three deliveries. Kallis, considered one of the game's greatest all-rounders, didn't panic as he stood at the top of his mark, but simply watched as Faulkner studied the field. 'I had a plan and I knew I could execute it,' Kallis said.

Before Kallis bowled each of his deliveries, he expected Faulkner would attempt the ramp shot—the unorthodox stroke in which the batsman flicks the ball behind him and to the boundary. It's as spectacular a shot as it is risky, something Faulkner must have realised when he attempted to scoop Kallis's fourth ball past wicketkeeper Chris Hartley. With 4 runs needed, he . . . missed the ball.

'I thought he might try that at some stage,' said Kallis, after joking that the excitement of the Thunder's 1-run victory was too much for a 40-year-old. 'When it's back of a length, it's quite difficult to hit that ramp shot. Again I backed myself and thought, "If he's going to try that, I'm going to make it as difficult as possible for him rather than being full in his zone where it's easy to play." '

A TWO-MAN TEAM

Perth Scorchers v
Melbourne Renegades
Etihad Stadium, 30 December 2015

The dynamic duo, Michael Klinger and Shaun Marsh, tick off another run as they guided Perth to a historic 10-wicket win over the Renegades.

Getty Images

After being set 171 runs to win by the Melbourne Renegades, Perth Scorchers openers Shaun Marsh and Michael Klinger tore up the record books in running down the score with eight deliveries to spare. While they fell 2 runs short of breaking the partnership record set by Melbourne Stars duo Luke Wright and Rob Quiney—that was simply because they ran out of runs to score. But the dynamic duo made Perth the first BBL team to launch a successful chase without losing a wicket.

With Renegades pace ace James Pattinson unavailable due to Test duties, Klinger was untroubled by the attack and scored an accomplished 90 from 58 deliveries. Marsh, who'd spent the previous four days as Australia's 12th man during the Boxing Day Test, needed only 54 balls to hammer his forceful 76.

Apart from two deliveries Marsh lofted to the leg side during the powerplay—both of which fell safely between the fielders—it was a faultless performance by both men. They ran roughshod over the bowlers, storming to 86 runs after 10 overs. With 42 balls remaining they needed only 57 runs to win.

While Klinger's performance emphasised his reliability, Marsh built upon his other dominant BBL performances in Melbourne, which included 79 from 51 against the Stars in BBL|04 and an unconquered 99 off 52 deliveries against the Renegades in BBL|01.

The loss was a bitter pill for the Renegades to swallow. 'It wasn't a case of someone tearing us apart, and all of the bowlers were looking at our shoelaces and hoping the skipper doesn't bowl us,' said Chris Tremain. 'Everyone was keen to get into the contest. We were met by two players who had an answer for everything we threw at them.'

The foundations of Etihad Stadium shook when Trent Lawford and Tom Beaton collided during a hard fought match between the Sixers and Renegades

FOOTY FEVER GRIPS THE BBL

Sydney Sixers v Melbourne Renegades Etihad Stadium, 23 December 2015

When Sixers fast bowler Trent Lawford—a giant of a man who strains the scales at 125 kilograms—and Melbourne Renegades batter Tom Beaton collided rugby-league-style at Etihad Stadium, it was a mismatch of David and Goliath proportions.

Beaton dropped a rising ball at his feet and scrambled through for a quick single, but the powerfully built Lawford veered across Beaton's path to retrieve the ball and the batter charged into Lawford's meaty left shoulder. If having his teeth rattled in the collision hadn't annoyed the batter enough, he must have been furious when Lawford's shot at the non-striker's-end stumps branded him between the shoulder blades.

Sixers skipper Moises Henriques conceded a football-like physicality was becoming part of the BBL, suggesting the collision highlighted that players were battling for every run. 'It shows how intense it is,' he said. 'The players are fighting for every run and you have to use your shoulder, use your body. It often happens with a bowler, when a ball gets hit back down the wicket and he tries to get in front of the non-striker to get the ball first. It was good to see Lawford get out and attack the ball.'

While Henriques doesn't condone physical contact in cricket, he insisted that Lawford—who was granted leave from his job on a building site to play in the BBL—was aiming for the stumps. 'It looked to me that if Trent had've hit the stumps, then [Beaton] would've been out,' he said. 'He got into the line of the throw, but I don't think he changed direction to get into that line. He just ran smart.'

Melbourne Stars' duo Scott Boland (far left) and John Hastings produced some 'death' bowling that left high profile teammate Kevin Pietersen in raptures.

BOWLED AND THE BEAUTIFUL

Melbourne Stars v Hobart Hurricanes
MCG, 6 January 2016

Batsmen normally dominate the headlines in the BBL, but Stars bowlers John Hastings and Scott Boland bucked that trend when they provided a masterclass to bowl out the final four overs of the innings against Hobart.

Former England batsman Kevin Pietersen, who has played in more than 500 limited-overs matches, paid the pair the ultimate compliment after Hobart, who were cruising at 4–98 with five overs remaining, were skittled for 124. 'That is the best death bowling by two bowlers I have seen in my whole career,' a stunned Pietersen told Network Ten after his team's 8-wicket triumph.

The Hurricanes batters could only scratch together 23 runs, as they were subjected to a relentless salvo of yorkers and tight bowling that seemed to petrify them. 'They did not miss a single yorker,' said Pietersen. 'I've just been chatting to [Hobart's West Indian import] Darren Sammy, and he said that is the best yorker bowling he's faced in his career. You don't often get two bowlers nailing 24 yorkers in a row, not giving a batsman one ball to hit.'

The pair also won high praise from the television commentators, former internationals Damien Fleming and Adam Gilchrist. They marvelled at the line and length that suffocated the Hurricanes' lower order. 'It [the yorker] is still a very good go-to delivery,' said Fleming, while Gilchrist called the performance as good as a cricket fan could ever see.

GLOSSARY

ALL-ROUNDER: A player who can bat and bowl at a sufficient standard to ensure selection in the team as a specialist in either role.

APPEAL: When the fielding side asks the umpire if a batsman is out. They normally yell 'Howzat!' as in 'How is that?'.

BAILS: Two pegs held horizontally in grooves at the top of the stumps. Together, the stumps and bails form a wicket and it must be broken (the bails dislodged) for a batsman to be dismissed.

BALL: White for Twenty20 and one-dayers, red or pink for first-class matches. It weighs 5.5 ounces (156 grams) in men's competition (5 oz/142 grams in the women's game) and is colloquially known as a 'rock'.

BLOCK: A defensive shot the batsman uses to preserve his wicket.

BOUNCER: A short-pitched ball used by the bowler to intimidate the batsman.

BOUNDARY: Two meanings: (a) the perimeter of a cricket field; and (b) a score of four if the ball hits the ground before leaving the field, or six if it goes over the boundary on the full.

BOWLED: The batsman is out bowled if the ball, either straight from the bowler's hand or via the batsman's bat or body, hits his wicket and dislodges at least one bail.

BOWLER: The person who delivers the cricket ball down the pitch to the batsman.

BYE: A run scored when the batsman doesn't touch the ball with either his bat or body. It's credited to sundries or extras and not the batsman's score.

CAUGHT: A batsman is given out caught when a fielder catches a ball he hits before it touches the ground.

CENTURY: The term used when a batsman scores 100 runs.

DUCK: A score of zero.

DUCKWORTH–LEWIS: The system devised by mathematicians Frank Duckworth and Tony Lewis to help decide limited-overs matches if they're interrupted by rain.

ECONOMY RATE (ECON): The average number of runs a bowler concedes per over.

EXTRAS/SUNDRIES: Runs that aren't scored by batsmen. The four common extras are byes, leg byes, wides and no balls.

FULL TOSS: A ball that reaches the batsmen without bouncing.

GOLDEN DUCK: When the batsman is dismissed by the first ball he faces.

HAT-TRICK: Three wickets taken by a bowler in successive balls.

INFIELD: The area of the ground inside the 30-yard (27.4-metre) circle.

INNINGS: Two meanings: (a) the time a batsman spends at the wicket until he's given out; and (b) the entire batting team's effort, ending when either 10 batsmen are dismissed or the captain declares his side's innings closed.

INSWING: When the ball swings in towards the batsmen.

LEG BEFORE WICKET (LBW): A batsman is out lbw if he's hit on his body or equipment and the umpire believes the ball would've hit the stumps.

LEG BREAK/SPIN: When the ball pitches and turns from leg to off for a right-hander.

LEG BYE: When the ball deflects off the batsman's body or equipment and the batsmen run. The batter must have offered a shot and leg byes don't count against the bowler.

LEG SIDE: The half of the ground behind the batsman's legs.

MIDDLE: Two meanings: (a) the centre of the field; and (b) a commentator might say the batsman 'middled it' when he strikes the ball with the meat of the bat.

NO BALL: When a bowler bowls an illegal delivery—either as a result of his arm action or if his foot lands over the popping crease—the umpire will rule a no ball. The bowler must bowl another ball and the batting team has a run added to its score. In limited-overs cricket a no ball is called if the ball passes the batter above shoulder height or if a ball from a seam bowler reaches the batsman on the full and at waist height.

OFF SIDE: The half of the ground towards which the batsman's feet are pointing.

ON SIDE: The same as the leg side.

OUT/DISMISSED: There are 10 possible ways of being dismissed: bowled, caught, run out, lbw, stumped, hit wicket, handled the ball, hit the ball twice, obstruction and timed out.

OUTFIELD: The area between the infield and the boundary. Even if a shot hit into the outfield goes straight to a fielder, it's far enough for the batsmen to run a single.

OUTSWING: When the ball swings away from the batsman and towards the slips.

PINCH-HITTERS: Lower-order batsmen promoted in the line-up to hit some quick runs. They're most often used when a team is chasing a big total in limited-overs matches.

PITCH: Two meanings: (a) the strip in the centre of the field where the batsmen face the bowlers; and (b) a way of describing the bounce of the ball: 'It pitches on a good length.'

POPPING CREASE: The line parallel to and 4 feet (1.2 metres) in front of the stumps at or behind which the batsman stands to face a ball.

RUN RATE: The average number of runs scored per over, or the number of runs per over a team needs to score in order to win a match.

RUN-UP: The strides a bowler takes as he moves in to deliver the ball.

SHOULDER ARMS: When a batsman, rather than risk being dismissed by a ball, lifts the bat high above his shoulders to keep his bat and hands out of harm's way.

SITTER: The easiest catch a fielder can hope to receive.

SLEDGING: A tactic the fielding team might use to try to unsettle a batsman or attempt to make him lose his concentration. It can be amusing or offensive banter.

SLOG: A shot that isn't in the coaching book.

SLOGGER: An exponent of the slog.

TAILENDER: A batsman who comes in towards the end of an innings and isn't noted for his batting prowess.

TWELFTH MAN: A substitute fielder. He can be called upon to field but isn't allowed to bat or bowl.

WIDE: A delivery that pitches too far away from the batsman and is impossible to score off. An extra is added to the batting team's total and the ball must be bowled again.

YORKER: A full-pitched delivery that's aimed at either the batsman's toes or the base of the stumps.

ABBREVIATIONS

*	NOT OUT
AV	AVERAGE
BBI	BEST BOWLING IN AN INNINGS
C	CAPTAIN
ECON	ECONOMY (RUNS PER OVER BOWLED)
HS	HIGHEST SCORE
S/R	STRIKE RATE
V	VERSUS

WHAT YOU NEED TO KNOW ABOUT BBL/WBBL GAMES

THE LOWDOWN

- The only difference between the BBL and WBBL playing field is the boundary size; the WBBL has a maximum boundary of 60 metres.
- Matches take three hours.
- The team with the most runs wins.
- Runs are scored by either running between the wickets or hitting boundaries.
- Each team gets to face 20 overs.
- The new batter must be at the crease within 90 seconds of their teammate being dismissed.
- The fielding team is only allowed to have two players outside the inner circle during the first six overs of an innings.
- At the end of six overs, another three players can join them outside the inner circle.
- Bowlers can bowl a maximum of four overs each. Each over consists of six balls, but if a bowler bowls a front-foot no ball (when no part of his or her front foot lands behind the crease), the batting team gets 1 free run and the batter gets a free hit, meaning they can't get out on that delivery.

THE SUPER OVER

- **If the scores are level at the end of 20 overs, each team will face one super over.**
- **The team that scores the most runs will be declared the winner. If, however, both teams finish the super over on the same score, the game will be declared a tie.**

THE POINTS TABLE

- Each BBL team plays eight games. WBBL teams play 14 games so they play one another twice before the semi final.
- The top four teams are decided by points. Two points are awarded for a win; when games finish in a tie or no result (for example, through rain) both teams will receive one point.
- If teams are equal on the points table, they'll be separated depending on their net run rate.

THE RUN RATE

- The run rate is the average runs per over a team scores (if a team scores 8 runs from 2 overs their run rate is 4). A team's net run rate is the difference between their run rate and that of their opposition. For example, the Heat are playing the Strikers. If the Heat have a run rate of 4 at the conclusion of their innings and the Strikers have a run rate of 3 at the end of their innings, the Heat's net run rate is 1 while the Strikers' net run rate is minus 1.
- Net run rates from each match are added at the completion of each match, and that figure is used to separate teams tied on points.

THE FINALS

- At the end of the regular season, the top four teams will play in the finals series.
- In the first semi final, the first-placed team will play the fourth-placed team. In the second semi final the second-placed team will play the third-placed team.
- The team that has finished highest in qualifying for each of the semi finals is rewarded with a home final.
- The winners of each semi final will square off in the Big Final.

ACKNOWLEDGEMENTS

I would like to offer my sincere thanks to a number of people for their efforts towards this, the second *Big Bash Book* project.

First, thank you to the BBL players, especially those who feature in this book. While every endeavour was made to speak directly to those players, in some instances it was necessary to source information from previously published articles, video interviews and/or by talking to their teammates for their insights into what makes them great players.

I also thank the BBL's media liaison officers—including Calum Young (Adelaide Strikers), Stephen Gray (Brisbane Heat), Eve Curley (Hobart Hurricanes), Hamish Jones (Melbourne Renegades), Cassie O'Brien (Melbourne Stars), Ben Somerford (Perth Scorchers), Jodie Hawkins (Sydney Sixers), and Chris Botherway and Simon Anderson (Sydney Thunder)—for their assistance. And I offer Mal Conn from Cricket New South Wales a special vote of thanks for arranging for me to travel around Australia to cover both Sydney teams' BBL campaigns. Sincere thanks, too, to a number of journalists whose superb coverage of BBL|05 and other cricket-related stories proved an invaluable resource while researching this book.

I thank Tom Gilliatt and the Allen & Unwin team for their constant enthusiasm and support. I'm especially indebted to Christa Munns and Nicola Young, whose professionalism and eye for detail is second to none.

Last but not least, I offer my wife Camille the biggest thanks for her patience throughout this innings.

Daniel Lane

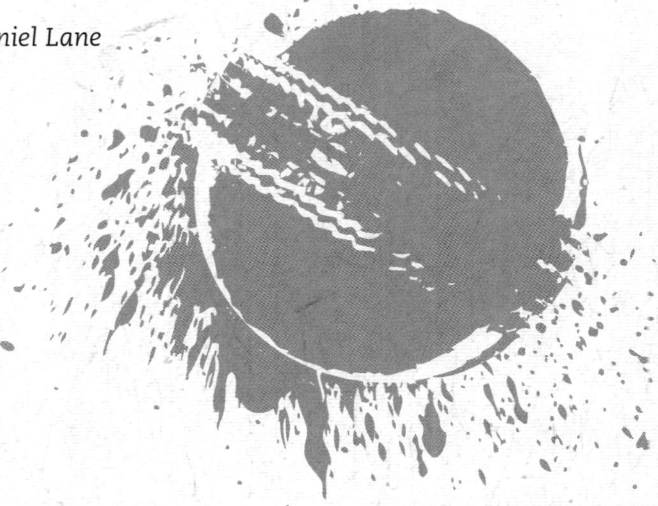

First published in 2016

Allen & Unwin
83 Alexander Street
Crows Nest NSW 2065
Australia
Phone: (61 2) 8425 0100
Email: info@allenandunwin.com
Web: www.allenandunwin.com

Cataloguing-in-Publication details are available
from the National Library of Australia
www.trove.nla.gov.au

ISBN 978 1 76029 141 9

Design by transformer.com.au, Sydney
Printed in Australia by Australian Book Connection

10 9 8 7 6 5 4 3 2 1